1991

Problems and Prospe
in Continuing
Professional Education

Ronald M. Cervero, Craig L. Scanlan, *Editors*

NEW DIRECTIONS FOR CONTINUING EDUCATION
GORDON G. DARKENWALD, *Editor-in-Chief*
ALAN B. KNOX, Consulting Editor

Number 27, September 1985

Jossey-Bass Inc., Publishers
San Francisco • London

OCT 2 1 1985

Ronald M. Cervero, Craig L. Scanlan (Eds.).
Problems and Prospects in Continuing Professional Education.
New Directions for Continuing Education, no. 27.
San Francisco: Jossey-Bass, 1985.

New Directions for Continuing Education
Gordon G. Darkenwald, *Editor-in-Chief*
Alan B. Knox, *Consulting Editor*

New Directions for Continuing Education (publication number USPS
493-930) is published quarterly by Jossey-Bass Inc., Publishers. Second class
postage rates paid at San Francisco, California, and at additional mailing
offices.

Correspondence:
Subscriptions, single-issue orders, change of address notices, undelivered
copies, and other correspondence should be sent to Subscriptions,
Jossey-Bass Inc., Publishers, 433 California Street, San Francisco,
California 94104.

Editorial correspondence should be sent to the managing Editor-
in-Chief, Gordon G. Darkenwald, Graduate School of Education,
Rutgers University, 10 Seminary Place, New Brunswick, New Jersey
08903.

Library of Congress Catalog Card Number 85-60828

International Standard Serial Number ISSN 0195-2242

International Standard Book Number ISBN 87589-745-2

Cover art by WILLI BAUM

Manufactured in the United States of America

Ordering Information

The paperback sourcebooks listed below are published quarterly and can be ordered either by subscription or single-copy.

Subscriptions cost $40.00 per year for institutions, agencies, and libraries. Individuals can subscribe at the special rate of $30.00 per year *if payment is by personal check.* (Note that the full rate of $40.00 applied if payment is by institutional check, even if the subscription is designated for an individual.) Standing orders are accepted.

Single copies are available at $9.95 when payment accompanies order, and *all single-copy orders under $25.00 must include payment.* (California, New Jersey, New York, and Washington, D.C., residents please include appropriate sales tax.) For billed orders, cost per copy is $9.95 plus postage and handling. (Prices subject to change without notice.)

Bulk orders (ten or more copies) of any individual sourcebook are available at the following discounted prices: 10-49 copies, $8.95 each; 50-00 copies, $7.96 each; over 100 copies, *inquire.* Sales tax and postage and handling charges apply as for single copy orders.

To ensure correct and prompt delivery, all orders must give either the *name of an individual* or an *official purchase order number.* Please submit your order as follows:

Subscriptions: specify series and year subscription is to begin.
Single Copies: specify sourcebook code (such as, CE1) and first two words of title.

Mail orders for United States and Possessions, Latin America, Canada, Japan, Australia, and New Zealand to:
Jossey-Bass Inc., Publishers
433 California Street
San Francisco, California 94104

Mail orders for all other parts of the world to:
Jossey-Bass Limited
28 Banner Street
London EC1Y 8QE

New Directions for Continuing Education Series
Gordon G. Darkenwald, *Editor-in-Chief*
Alan B. Knox, *Consulting Editor*

Contents

Editors' Notes

Throughout the last three decades, continuing professional education has undergone tremendous growth and diversification. As is natural during periods of rapid expansion, the tendency has been to focus efforts on providing more and better services. The resulting activity has made it easy to overlook a concomitant increase both in the number and in the complexity of the issues now facing the field.

This sourcebook is based on the premise that the directions that continuing professional education will take in the future can be determined only by careful and deliberate consideration of the problems and prospects that it now faces. The contributors to this volume, experienced practitioners, policy makers, and scholars in continuing education, have identified what they believe to be the most salient issues confronting the field and provided the perspectives necessary to begin addressing its future.

That many of the major issues characterizing continuing professional education remain unresolved can be attributed in part to an absence of clarity regarding its goals and purposes. In Chapter One, Scanlan uses a historical analysis of the field to clarify its various aims. He presents and discusses a goal orientations model that may prove useful in addressing both programmatic and policy considerations.

Changing perspectives on the nature of professionalism and on the focus of continuing professional education interventions are altering our assumptions about the role that continuing professional educators can, do, and should assume. In Chapter Two, Cervero, Bussigel, and Hellyer apply both traditional and emerging viewpoints in order to clarify these perspectives and examine their impact on the relationships between educational practitioners and the professions.

Increasing the responsiveness and quality of continuing professional education and addressing its current and evolving policy issues require better understanding of those who participate in our programming, namely the professionals themselves. A knowledge of professionals' reasons for participation in continuing education is particularly useful in this regard. In Chapter Three, Grotelueschen describes recent developments in the study of professionals' participation and presents an approach that holds substantial promise for improving practice, policy making, and research.

Internal and external demands for quality assurance in continuing professional education have caused program and provider accreditation standards to proliferate. In Chapter Four, Kenny explores the tasks and challenges confronting continuing educators responsible for planning and

1

developing programming that is consistent with professional expectations. Continuing educators are increasingly being expected to manage both education and information effectively. Developing complementary skills in these two areas is essential if educators are to assume leadership in the field.

Of and by themselves, external standards provide an insufficient basis for informed decision making. In Chapter Five, Knox places the issue of evaluating continuing professional education in perspective. Careful analysis of the role, purposes, and methods of educational evaluation provides a framework for efforts to enhance the use of information in planning, improving, and justifying our program efforts. Knox pays special attention to assessing self-directed learning efforts and to measuring the impact of continuing professional education on practice.

The increasing tendency of organizations to plan, develop, and implement programming collaboratively represents a major new direction for continuing professional education. In Chapter Six, Hohmann assesses the trends that have precipitated the increase in joint efforts. She uses a case study to delineate and explain factors contributing to successful linkage arrangements.

Collaborative sponsorship arrangements have heightened continuing educators' awareness of the frequency with which rights, obligations, and values come into conflict. In Chapter Seven, Scanlan identifies the major sources of values conflict for continuing professional education and shows how principles or moral reasoning can be used to resolve some ethical dilemmas commonly encountered in practice.

In Chapter Eight, Griffith reviews the problems and prospects addressed in the preceding chapters in the context of four key questions: First, who are continuing professional educators? Second, whose learning do they plan, guide, and evaluate? Third, on what content should this learning focus? Fourth, how should this learning be accomplished? These four questions are discussed within the framework of the diverse purposes that continuing professional educators attempt to serve. Thus, Griffith brings us back to the point from which we began, addressing our need to define who we are, what we do, and why we do it.

The purpose of this sourcebook is to provide continuing educators, policy makers, and scholars with the perspectives necessary to address these issues with clarity and foresight. To the extent that its chapters prove enabling, the authors' intentions will be realized.

Ronald M. Cervero
Craig L. Scanlan
Editors

Ronald M. Cervero, former assistant director of the Illinois Council on Continuing Medical Education, is associate professor of adult and continuing education in the Department of Leadership and Educational Policy Studies at Northern Illinois University, DeKalb. His current research interests include the relationship between continuing professional education and practitioner performance, professionals' modes of learning, and professionalization.

Craig L. Scanlan is chairman of the Department of Health Education, Evaluation, and Research in the School of Health-Related Professions at the University of Medicine and Dentistry of New Jersey, Newark. His current research interests include participation in continuing professional education, professionalization and professional ethics, accreditation, and goal-based evaluation.

*Reflective consideration of what we do and why we do
it can provide sound direction to practice.*

Practicing with Purpose:
Goals of Continuing
Professional Education

Craig L. Scanlan

Continuing professional education has rightly been characterized as a disorderly market (Stern, 1983). Both within its disciplines and across its disciplines, there are wide variations in the focus, content, and methods of its delivery. Like many other movements in education, "everyone has gotten on the bandwagon, but not everyone is playing the same tune" (Kempfer, 1979, p. 23). The diversity is due in part to the wide range of purposes, goals, and objectives ascribed to continuing professional education. Indeed, like continuing education in general, continuing professional education has no single underlying framework, no single set of basic assumptions and principles from which all involved can view the field (Darkenwald and Merriam, 1982).

Much of the diversity of educational purpose reflects the pluralism of our society as a whole. Although Diekhoff's (cited in White, 1970, p. 122) assessment of this diversity is now two decades old and although it was directed to the continuing education community at large, it remains germane for those responsible for continuing professional education: "As long as we are a pluralistic society, as long as our public is made up of many publics, we shall continue to have philosophies of education in

R. M. Cervero, C. L. Scanlan (Eds.). *Problems and Prospects in Continuing Professional Education.* New Directions
for Continuing Education, no. 27. San Francisco: Jossey-Bass, September 1985.

conflict with one another. Meanwhile, educators will continue to muddle along as best they can (which is very well indeed) on the basis of different philosophies (or different assumptions), often not formulated at all; and they will continue to feel pressure from different individuals and publics with varied philosophies and assumptions. It has been said that the United States does not have an ideology; it is one. The same may be said of American education. Like the American ideology, the philosophy of education is tentative, changing, and eclectic."

Intrinsic differences among the professions themselves further increase the diversity in purposes, goals, and objectives characterizing continuing professional education. Houle (1980) and Knox (1968) have identified commonalities in educational needs, resources, and methods across professional groups, but they both also knowledge occupational claims to unique expertise and distinctive traditions. Moreover, the professions exhibit substantial diversity in both the settings characterizing their practice and in the point of view, outlook, or assumptions underlying such practice (Houle, 1980).

The pragmatic orientation characterizing most continuing professional education compounds the effects of societal pluralism and professional differences. Like continuing educators in general, those responsible for the provision of continuing professional education are too often concerned more with what to do than with why they should do it (Roberts, 1976). Indeed, the emphasis on skills rather than principles, on means rather than ends, and on details rather than the big picture probably increases the confusion over the goals and purposes of continuing education (Darkenwald and Merriam, 1982).

This confusion is problematic. Without a clear perspective on the aims of continuing professional education, it is little wonder that providers and participants alike are often confused about the nature of their roles. The absence of clarity on the goals and purposes of continuing professional education can also create artificial barriers to cooperation between and among professional groups. In the absence of a coherent goals framework, many of the major issues and questions surrounding continuing professional education are destined to remain muddled and unresolved.

Identifying the various goals characterizing continuing professional education can help to place questions about what is, why it is, and what it should be in proper perspective, thereby giving sound and purposeful direction to practice (Apps, 1973). Moreover, reflective consideration of what we do and of why we do it can provide the necessary framework for examining our key assumptions regarding learners, providers, and the content and process of continuing education (Merriam, 1977). Finally, inquiry into the purposes of continuing education can help to clarify many of its major issues (for example, mandatory participation, effectiveness) and ultimately to provide the basis for more rational and coherent policy making (Darkenwald and Merriam, 1982). If, as some have charged, the field of continuing professional education is in a state of sprawling disarray (Stern, 1983), the solution may well lie in infusing its institutions with a better sense of purpose.

Philosophical Framework

The purposes that an individual or institution ascribes to continuing education activities are an outgrowth of values, beliefs, and principles underlying educational practice. When such a combination of assumptions and dispositions is applied to practical ends, it constitutes what Apps (1973) calls one's working philosophy.

The need to incorporate philosophical consideration into the continuing professional education planning process has long been recognized (Hutchinson, 1974), and most practitioners of continuing professional education make their decisions and fulfill their roles in ways that presuppose certain values and beliefs. Nonetheless, the field has generally failed to grapple with the assumptions underlying its practice, and it has yet to elaborate fully a working philosophy.

Adult Education Perspective. Fortunately, the literature on continuing education provides direction. In contrast to the literature on continuing professional education, the literature on continuing education has a long tradition of philosophical inquiry (Knowles, 1957; Lindeman, 1961; Kallen, 1962; Bergevin, 1967, Lawson, 1975; Elias and Merriam, 1980). Given the close relationship between continuing education and continuing professional education, such inquiry provides a useful foundation for reflective consideration of the goals, purposes, and assumptions currently underlying continuing professional education.

Apps's (1973) synthesis of extant educational philosophies provided a framework for analysis of the values, beliefs, and principles underlying continuing education practice. Applying the assumptions characterizing the five major movements in educational philosophy, Apps derived a typology of three continuing education learning models, each oriented toward a different goal (Figure 1). According to this framework, the essentialist-perennialist model aims to assist learners in acquiring content and mastering facts and information, the progressivist-reconstructionist perspective seeks to develop individual or communal problem-solving capacities, and the existentialist orientation attempts to guide learners toward personal self-actualization. Assumptions regarding the role of the learner, the role of the provider, and the function of content differ with the goal espoused.

Elaborating on the frameworks of Apps and other scholars (Kohlberg and Mayer, 1972; Elias and Merriam, 1980), Darkenwald and Merriam (1982) identified five major aims of adult education: to cultivate the intellect, to facilitate individual self-fulfillment, to promote personal and socie-

Figure 1. Apps's Typology of Continuing Education Learning Models

	Essentialist-Perennialist	Progressivist-Reconstructionist	Existentialist
Goal	Acquiring content	Problem solving	Self-actualization
Role of Learner	Recipient of content	Problem solver	Self-searching
Role of Provider	Translator, communication link	Helper, knowledge source	Guide and counselor
Function of Content	An end	A means	A means

Source: Apps, 1973.

tal improvement, to catalyze social transformation, and to advance organizational effectiveness. Like Apps, Darkenwald and Merriam insist that one's perceptions regarding the learner, provider, content, and process of education are contingent on one's goal orientations.

Application to Continuing Professional Education. Although the various philosophical perspectives emerging from the continuing education literature are not fully generalizable, they do help to explain current ambiguities over the purposes and methods of continuing professional education. Diversity of purpose is explained in part by the fact that the selection of educational goals is a normative process; the goals that one ascribes to continuing professional education, like the goals that one ascribes to continuing education, depend on one's underlying values and beliefs. Moreover, the literature acknowledges diversity of method as the logical extension of diverse purposes; one's approach to the learner, provider, content, and process of continuing professional education varies with the goals that one has chosen.

Bringing order out of chaos requires more than simply acknowledging diversity. Besides helping to explain the eclectic nature of continuing professional education, the literature does much to clarify its purposes. Two of the most important insights emerging from the philosophical literature are the distinction between means and ends and the differentiation of purpose according to intended beneficiaries.

The distinction between means and ends differentiates between the instrumental and intrinsic values ascribed to continuing education. The instrumental perspective views continuing education as a means to a particular end, for example, remediation, growth, or change. This utilitarian focus is most evident in progressivist and reconstructionist thought. In contrast to this viewpoint, the intrinsic orientation values education as an end in itself. Based in part on essentialist and perennialist philosophies, the intrinsic values orientation seeks no pragmatic justification for learning; indeed, cultivation of the intellect is valued for its own sake, independent of individual, organizational, or social goals.

The differentiation of the intended beneficiaries of continuing education that one encounters in the literature further helps to clarify the methods and purposes ascribed to continuing professional education. Whereas the individual orientation has long pervaded continuing education, its potential role in organizations and the social system is now receiving increased attention. This expanded conception of purpose can be attributed in part to the growing acceptance of the utilitarian perspective as the dominant ideology of continuing education. These changing orientations are clearly evident in the evolution of continuing professional education.

Evaluation of Purpose in Continuing Professional Education

The emergence of various goals orientations in the continuing education of professionals tends to parallel the general development of the professions themselves. Although the actual time lines vary according to the developmental stage of the individual professions, the overall trends are remarkably similar. The variations that do occur are based mainly on differences in professionals' practice settings and in the point of view, outlook, or assumptions underlying such practice.

Intrinsic Values Orientation. The priests of primitive society, the guild members of medieval times, and those entering the learned occupations after study in the post-Renaissance universities of Europe all took the need for continuing learning for granted (Houle, 1983). The knowledge underlying the practice of these original professionals, albeit rudimentary by today's standards, was founded on theories then current in the basic arts and sciences. Implicit in the elaboration of such theory was the ongoing search for basic truths, that is, knowledge for the sake of knowledge. As the traditional professions established their collective identity, intellectual inquiry became firmly entrenched as both an intrinsic occupational value and as a desired characteristic of those aspiring to professional status. That our modern conception of professionalism still embodies the value of ongoing inquiry attests to the persistence of this early orientation toward continuing learning. Felch (1981, p. 3) has emphasized the importance of this tradition for the profession of medicine: "Physicians having the right mindset—the unremitting attitude of intellectual curiosity—practice medical education that is truly continuing." Although the intrinsic values orientation, with its emphasis on rigorous self-directed inquiry and the development and synthesis of basic knowledge (often spanning many disciplinary areas) lives on among the more innovative members of our modern professions (Houle, 1980), its influence seems to be waning. George Pickering (cited by Ellis, 1978, p. 513) decried the loss of scholarly habits as the central tragedy of contemporary medical education: "Such habits have made medicine into a highly respected learned profession, and only the possession of such habits will keep it so." The parallels with other professions are clear.

Instrumental Perspective. The eighteenth and nineteenth centuries represented a period of dramatic change for both society and the evolving professions. With the age of rationality came growing demands for pragmatic solutions to emerging social problems. With the industrial revolution came an increasing emphasis on applied technical knowledge and specialization. Within this milieu, the professions strengthened their hold over their distinctive knowledge bases and increasingly emphasized the utility of content, skills, and principles applied to practical ends.

Remediating Deficiences. Ironically, the explosive growth of applied knowledge itself posed a significant problem to the professions, a problem to which continuing education was first applied as a practical solution. In the early twentieth century, formal programs of postgraduate continuing education were established to remediate the shortcomings then characterizing medicine's basic professional education system (Shepard, 1960). Similar compensatory adjustments (Flexner, 1910) were applied in such professions as librarianship, where a large proportion of the early work force lacked the formal education that its members needed to fulfill their roles (Hiatt, 1979). The reparative orientation of continuing education is still evident today in such professions as law, where "bridging-the-gap" courses fill the void between theory-oriented basic education and practical applications (Bushman, 1976).

As many of the professions developed mechanisms to strengthen their basic educational preparation (for example, practicums and internships) and to ensure that neophytes were indeed fit for the responsibilities of practice (for example, state licensure, professional credentialing), the focus of continuing education shifted from remediation of deficiencies in prior education to correction of the gaps in knowledge and skills that practicing professionals increasingly encountered as they attempted to keep abreast of new developments in their fields (Bushman, 1976; Chamberlain, 1976; Hiatt, 1979; Shepard, 1960). As the pace of knowledge acquisition quickened, old principles and methods were rapidly abandoned. In many disciplines, professional obsolescence became an occupational hazard to which continuing education was applied as the cure (Dubin, 1971). The notion of continuing education as a remedial treatment for obsolete knowledge and skills still dominates the ideology of the technically oriented professions, such as engineering (Siefert, 1963; Mali, 1970).

With the acknowledgement that professional knowledge and skills were subject to obsolescence came the recognition that not all practitioners were either willing or able to maintain the level of proficiency necessary to deliver competent services. This realization became particularly evident among the client-oriented professions, especially those responsible for the delivery of health services. In a telling observation made some fifty years ago, the Commission on Medical Education (quoted by Shepard, 1960, p. 743) concluded that "the time may come when every physician may be required in the public interest to take continuation courses to ensure that his practice will be kept abreast of current methods of diagnosis, treatment, and prevention."

It was not until the 1960s that such a shift in the orientation toward continuing professional education occurred. During this period, which Houle (1983) has called the second era of continuing professional education, a confluence of public pressure, governmental intervention, and professional acquiescence transformed a relatively simple system intended to facilitate professional updating into a complex mechanism designed to assure professionals' competence. Beginning with the health professions (medicine, dentistry, nursing, pharmacy, optometry, clinical psychology, and allied health), this competency assurance orientation to continuing education subsequently spread to other client-oriented professions. It now represents the dominant ideology among such diverse disciplines as public accountancy, law, real estate, nursing home administration, and social work. The impact of this orientation is clearly evident in the hundreds of state statutes now linking a professional's right to practice with mandated participation in continuing education activities (Phillips, 1983).

Although the competency assurance ideology represents an exponential leap in expectations, it has much in common with earlier remedial orientations to continuing education. All tend to emphasize gaps between existing and desired performance standards, and all translate these normative needs into remedial-behavioral approaches to learning. The most notable difference among these approaches is in regard to content. Whereas earlier remedial orientations focused mainly on knowledge deficiencies, the professional updating and competency assurance approaches have increasingly emphasized gaps in proficiency (the ability to perform) or actual performance deficits.

Fostering Growth. Early dissatisfaction and recent disillusionment with the limitations of the remedial approach to continuing professional education have prompted some leaders in the field to reconceptualize its role. The resulting reassessment is based on the growing recognition that a modern professional's career path is no longer linear and stable but marked by frequent and often complex changes in responsibilities, direction, or both. From this perspective, continuing education based solely on the remedial goals of updating knowledge or assuring minimal competence is clearly insufficient; both professional and personal growth and development must also be facilitated (Houle, 1980).

The growth orientation toward continuing education is most evident among professionals working in collective or hierarchical settings, such as nurses (Cooper and Hornback, 1973) and managerial personnel (Miller, 1976). In such settings, shifts in specialization, assumption of supervisory responsibilities, and promotion to higher levels of administrative authority represent common transitions in a professional's career line. These transitions require professionals to master new concepts and skills.

The growth orientation toward continuing professional education has also recognized the need for personal self-enhancement through the pursuit of knowledge, skills, and sensitivities not directly related to one's occupational role (Houle, 1980). This personal development perspective is intended to complement the professional growth orientation by providing professionals with opportunities to broaden the often narrow viewpoints that they bring to bear on their work roles. Although the personal development perspective is mainly utilitarian in focus, it comes closest to fulfilling the original intent of the intrinsic values orientation noted previously.

Whereas most remedial approaches to continuing professional education are normative in orientation, the growth perspective emphasizes the unique attributes of both the individual professional and his or her practice settings. Within the framework, learners assume an active role in cooperative partnership with providers, applying situational and problem-solving strategies appropriate to their needs, interests, and ambitions.

Facilitating Change. The professions, like society as a whole, are in a constant state of dynamic change. Changing social, economic, and political conditions; alterations in societal and professional values, norms, and expectations; and rapid advances in technology all have a dramatic impact on the role and functions of the modern professions. For the individual professional, such changes often demand significant reform in the nature of one's practice or in the very way in which one views the field. Such changes can cause a profession to make profound alterations in its delivery system or even to reconceptualize its collective mission (Houle, 1980). Continuing education is increasingly being applied to facilitate such change.

Although this approach is not yet as common as the remedial or growth orientations, it is often described in the literature on continuing professional education. Changes in the political and economic climate of the early 1970s necessitated massive reorientation of aerospace engineers to fulfill different roles in other technical specialties (Pigott, 1976). During the same period, changes in educational philosophy demanded widespread retraining of science teachers in process-oriented approaches to curriculum (Arons, 1976). Since then, various authors have proposed that continuing education can facilitate needed reforms in the delivery of library, mental health, and banking services (Hiatt, 1979; Chamberlain, 1976; Curran, 1983). Current applications of continuing professional education as an agent of change involve the legal profession's reformulation of ethical standards and medicine's ongoing reorientation toward health promotion and disease prevention.

Depending on its focus, change-oriented continuing professional education can employ conceptions of the learner, provider, content, and process of education similar to or different from those underlying the remedial and growth approaches. The conceptions depend in part on the intended target for change: individual, organization, or delivery system.

Intended Beneficiaries. As just noted, the instrumental goals of continuing professional education—remediating deficiencies, fostering growth, and facilitating change—can be further categorized according to the intended targets or beneficiaries of the educational effort.

The Individual Practitioner. Since the traditional conception of professional is one of an autonomous practitioner in an entrepreneurial setting, it is little wonder that, until recently, most continuing professional education was oriented to the individual. The individual orientation is not to be confused with individualized approaches to education. Indeed, the ideology that now dominates continuing professional education—the remedial approach—makes normative assumptions when identifying group needs, selecting educational methods, and evaluating learning outcomes. Of course, increased attention to the growth and change orientations is increasing the emphasis on truly individualized approaches to learning and its evaluation, as Knox's discussion of self-directed learning in Chapter Five shows.

The Organization. As the entrepreneurial mode of practice has become increasingly obsolete (Houle, 1980), the educational needs of professionals employed in organizational settings have received increasing attention. Although the unique and often conflicting dynamic between individual professional and organizational expectations has long been acknowledged (Corwin, 1965), only recently were the individual and organizational approaches toward continuing professional education clearly distinguished (Lauffer, 1977). For the individual orientation, intervention aims at the upgrading, improvement, or change in a professional's practice. In contrast, the organizational approach conceives of these impacts as intermediary steps toward a further end, namely increasing the effectiveness of the organization. In this context, the distinctions drawn by Nadler (1970) between an organization's training, education, and development activities closely parallel the assumptions underlying the deficiency, growth, and change orientations discussed in this chapter.

The Delivery System. A professional delivery system represents a complex combination of interacting structures and processes ultimately designed to provide service to a targeted group. Shareholders in a professional delivery system include the professionals themselves, their providing organizations, educational institutions, and collegial associations. Stakeholders in the system—those who provide the capital, have needs for the system, or make demands on it—include society as a whole, its individual members, and the government. A professional delivery system is effective to the extent that it meets the needs and expectations of its stakeholders. Thus, continuing education oriented toward correcting, improving, or changing a professional delivery system must recognize and address the needs and expectations of those who have a stake in its operation. Despite widespread acknowledgement of the need for such a broadened perspective (Houle, 1980), only dentistry formally requires continuing professional education providers to meet the needs and interests not only of the profession but of the public at large (American Dental Association, 1978). As Chapter Two shows, consideration of the social and structural elements of the professional delivery system can fundamentally alter our assumptions regarding the learner, provider, content, and process of continuing professional education.

Application to Practice

A review of the literature uncovers nine major goal orientations to continuing professional education. Each is based on different values, beliefs, and premises (Figure 2). Although the updating/competency assurance orientation (orientation 1) currently dominates continuing professional education practice all nine perspectives are operative in the field, and many providers subscribe to more than one approach.

Besides giving us an opportunity to conceptualize what we do and why we do it, examination of these various goal orientations can give sound direction to practice. The model displayed in Figure 2 has practical implications both for programmatic considerations and for policy considerations.

Programmatic Considerations. Program development should begin with careful consideration of purpose (Hutchinson, 1974). Subsequent planning, implementation, and evaluation activities should reflect the goal orientations selected and be consistent with their underlying assumptions. To clarify these important considerations, we will examine three different goal orientations to continuing education in an academic setting.

Identifying Purpose. Continuing education in the academic setting commonly falls into one or more of three major categories: faculty development, organizational development, and instructional development (Gaff, 1975). Although there is considerable overlap among these activities, each approach clearly represents a different goal orientation (Figure 3). Faculty development activities best exemplify the individual growth orientation (orientation 2). Organizational development activities clearly represent the organizational development orientation (orientation 6). Instructional development efforts, especially those designed to correct shortcomings in the

Figure 2. Goal Orientations of Continuing Professional Education

	Remediating Deficiencies	Fostering Growth	Facilitating Change
Individual	Orientation 1 Updating/ competency assurance	Orientation 2 Individual growth	Orientation 3 Professional reorientation
Organization	Orientation 4 Employee training	Orientation 5 Employee education	Orientation 6 Organizational development
System	Orientation 7 Systems deficit	Orientation 8 Systems improvement	Orientation 9 Systems reform

teaching-learning system, best characterize the systems deficit orientation (orientation 7).

Planning. Once a clear distinction is drawn among goal orientations, clear differences emerge in one's approach to planning. Under the assumptions of the individual growth orientation, the content of faculty development activities can be specified by individualized assessment of felt needs, interests, and ambitions. Needs assessment for organizational development focuses on objective determination of changes necessary to increase the effectiveness of the institution (unit, department) in achieving its overall goals, with major emphasis on its key shareholders, the faculty and the administration. The content underlying instructional development processes evolves from assessment of deficiencies in the teaching-learning system as determined in part by its key stakeholders, students.

Implementation. Implementation of faculty development activities would be heavily founded on principles of social and developmental psychology. It could be expected to include individual and collaborative group efforts to enhance the professional and personal growth of those involved through the provision of professional service, research, scholarship, or administrative learning opportunities. Implementation of organization development activities would be based on principles of organizational theory and include such methods as team building and action research. Implementation of instructional development activities would rely on the assumptions underlying educational systems theory and instructional technology and include remedial-behavioral approaches to learning.

Evaluation. Under the individual growth orientation, evaluation of faculty development efforts would use both objective indicators and self-assessments to assess individual faculty members' enhanced professional and personal capacities. Evaluation of organizational development activities

Figure 3. The Goal Orientations Model Applied to Continuing Education in the Academic Setting

	Faculty Development	*Organizational Development*	*Instructional Development*
Goal Orientation	Individual growth (orientation 2)	Organizational development (orientation 6)	Systems deficit (orientation 7)
Primary Stakeholders	Faculty	Administration	Students
Planning	Emphasis on felt needs of faculty	Emphasis on goals of organization	Emphasis on deficiencies in teaching-learning system
Implementation Concepts	Developmental psychology	Organizational theory	Educational systems theory (Behavioral)
Focus of Evaluation	Changes in personal or professional capacities of individual faculty	Effectiveness of institutional change/goal achievement	Multiple indicators of improvements in instructional system

Source: Gaff, 1975.

would strive to document the effectiveness of institutional change as progress toward the achievement of goals. Evaluation of instructional development efforts would use curricular materials, faculty teaching performance, student learning, and student satisfaction with instruction as multiple indicators of improvements in the teaching-learning system.

Policy Considerations. Many of the ambiguities involved in the formulation of policy on continuing professional education arise from the absence of clarity or consensus on goal orientations. Current debates over mandatory continuing education and effectiveness of continuing professional education are good examples.

Mandatory Continuing Education. The debate over mandatory continuing education represents a classic example of values in conflict. Those supporting mandatory continuing education for professionals base their arguments on the assumptions and premises underlying the remedial approaches to continuing professional education, that is, on goal orientations 1, 4, or 7. Those opposed to mandatory continuing education base their arguments on the values and principles inherent in the growth orientations to continuing professional education, that, on orientations 2, 5, or 8. The power or validity of opposing evidence notwithstanding, the debate will not be resolved unless or until the parties reach agreement on what constitutes the appropriate goal for continuing professional education. In the absence of such consensus, policy decisions regarding mandatory continuing education will continue to be based on political or economic considerations, not on fundamental values.

Effectiveness of Continuing Professional Education. Clear differentiation of the various goal orientations also helps to explain why both the research literature and the rhetoric on the effectiveness of continuing professional education present so many conflicting viewpoints. All too often, the measures used to assess the effectiveness or impact of continuing education are inconsistent with the premises underlying the goal orientation of the intervention being assessed. A classic example of such incongruency is the study by Lewis and Hassanein (1970) of the effectiveness of continuing medical education. Those researchers scrutinized the "traditional" continuing education offered by a medical school—traditional in the sense that it focused on the principles underlying the updating/competency assurance goal orientation (orientation 1). However, the measures of effectiveness chosen—incidence of specific procedures and mortality in the population—were more appropriate to assessing outcomes of the systems deficit orientation. Such flaws in problem definition are likely to persist as long as we are not clear about the premises underlying the various goal orientations toward continuing professional education. It is time that we stop asking unanswerable questions, such as is continuing professional education effective, and start addressing the validity of the model's components. For example, does continuing professional education based on the assumptions inherent in a given orientation achieve the goal intended?

Conclusion

As Kohlberg and Mayer (1972, p. 449) have stated, "the most important issue confronting educators and educational theorists is the choice of ends for the instructional process." This chapter has elaborated the various goal orientations currently characterizing continuing professional education and identified their practical implications. I hope that the model described here will assist continuing professional education practitioners to articulate their own working philosophies and ultimately to strengthen the links between purpose and practice.

References

American Dental Association, Council on Dental Education. *Standards for Approval of Institutions and Organizations Offering Continuing Dental Education Programs.* Chicago: American Dental Association, 1978.

Apps, J. W. *Toward a Working Philosophy of Adult Education.* Occasional Paper No. 36. Syracuse: Syracuse University Publications in Continuing Education, 1973.

Arons, A. "Science for In-service School Teachers I: The Need for Further Profes-

18

sional Development." In P. P. LeBreton (Ed.), *The Assessment and Development of Professionals: Theory and Practice*. Seattle: University of Washington, 1976.

Bergevin, P. *A Philosophy for Adult Education*. New York: Seabury Press, 1967.

Bushman, W. M. "Continuing Legal Education in the 1970s." In P. P. LeBreton (Ed.), *The Assessment and Development of Professionals: Theory and Practice*. Seattle: University of Washington, 1976.

Chamberlain, J. G. "A National Approach to Mental Health Continuing Education." In P. P. LeBreton (Ed.), *The Assessment and Development of Professionals: Theory and Practice*. Seattle: University of Washington, 1976.

Cooper, S. S., and Hornback, M. S. *Continuing Nursing Education*. New York: McGraw-Hill, 1973.

Corwin, R. G. "Professional Persons in Public Organizations." *Educational Administration Quarterly*, 1965, *1*, 1–22.

Curran, J. R. "The Professions in Banking." In M. R. Stern (Ed.), *Power and Conflict in Continuing Professional Education*. Belmont, Calif.: Wadsworth, 1983.

Darkenwald, G. G., and Merriam, S. B. *Adult Education: Foundation of Practice*. New York: Harper & Row, 1982.

Dubin, S. S. (Ed.). *Professional Obsolescence*. Lexington, Mass.: Lexington Books, 1971.

Elias, J., and Merriam, S. M. *Philosophical Foundations of Adult Education*. New York: Kreiger, 1980.

Ellis, J. R. "The Pickering Survey." *Lancet*, 1978, *2* (8088), 512–513.

Felch, W. C. "CME or EME?" *Alliance for Continuing Medical Education Almanac*, 1981, *3* (4), 3.

Flexner, A. *Medical Education in the United States and Canada*. New York: Carnegie Foundation for the Advancement of Teaching, 1910.

Gaff, J. G. *Toward Faculty Renewal: Advances in Faculty, Instructional, and Organizational Development*. San Francisco: Jossey-Bass, 1975.

Hiatt, P. "The Impact of Continuing Education on Library Change." In P. P. LeBreton and Associates (Eds.), *The Evaluation of Continuing Education for Professionals: A Systems View*. Seattle: University of Washington, 1979.

Houle, C. O. *Continuing Learning in the Professions*. San Francisco: Jossey-Bass, 1980.

Houle, C. O. "Possible Futures." In M. R. Stern (Ed.), *Power and Conflict in Continuing Professional Education*. Belmont, Calif.: Wadsworth, 1983.

Hutchinson, D. J. "The Process of Planning Programs of Continuing Education for Health Manpower." In A. N. Charters and R. J. Blakely (Eds.), *Fostering the Growing Need to Learn*. Washington, D. C.: U.S. Government Printing Office, 1974.

Kallen, H. M. *Philosophical Issues in Adult Education*. Springfield, Ill.: Thomas, 1962.

Kempfer, H. "What Is Continuing Education?" *Lifelong Learning: The Adult Years*, 1979, *11*, 23.

Knowles, M. S. "Philosophical Issues That Confront Adult Educators." *Adult Education*, 1957, *7*, 234–244.

Knox, A. B. *Emerging Directions in Continuing Professional Education*. New York: Teachers College, Columbia University, 1968.

Kohlberg, L., and Mayer, R. "Development as the Aim of Education." *Harvard Educational Review*, 1972, *42*, 449–496.

Lauffer, A. *The Practice of Continuing Education in the Human Services*. New York: McGraw-Hill, 1977.

Lawson, K. H. *Philosophical Concepts and Values in Adult Education.* Nottingham, England: Barnes and Humby, 1975.

Lewis, C. E., and Hassanein, R. S. "Continuing Medical Education: An Epidemiological Evaluation." *New England Journal of Medicine,* 1970, *282,* 254–259.

Lindeman, E. C. *The Meaning of Adult Education.* Montreal: Harvest House, 1961.

Mali, P. "Measurement of Obsolescence in Engineering Practitioners." *Continuing Education,* 1970, *3* (2), 57–59, 63.

Merriam, S. B. "Philosophical Perspectives on Adult Education: A Critical Review of the Literature." *Adult Education,* 1977, *17,* 195–208.

Miller, E. G. "Developing Managerial Capability in the Public Sector." In P. P. LeBreton (Ed.), *The Assessment and Development of Professionals: Theory and Practice.* Seattle: University of Washington, 1976.

Nadler, L. *Developing Human Resources.* Houston: Gulf, 1970.

Phillips, L. E. "Trends in State Licensure." In M. R. Stern (Ed.), *Power and Conflict in Continuing Professional Education.* Belmont, Calif.: Wadsworth, 1983.

Pigott, G. M. "The Effectiveness of a Short-Term Accelerated Programs for Reorienting Professionals." In P. P. LeBreton (Ed.), *The Assessment and Development of Professionals: Theory and Practice.* Seattle: University of Washington, 1976.

Roberts, H. W. "Goals, Objectives, and Functions in Adult Education." *Adult Education,* 1976, *26,* 123–129.

Shepard, C. R. "History of Continuing Medical Education in the United States Since 1930." *Journal of Medical Education,* 1960, *35,* 740–758.

Siefert, W. *The Prevention and Cure of Obsolescence in Scientific and Technical Personnel.* Philadelphia: Industrial Research Institute, 1963.

Stern, M. R. "A Disorderly Market." In M. R. Stern (Ed.), *Power and Conflict in Continuing Professional Education.* Belmont, Calif.: Wadsworth, 1983.

White, T. J. "Philosophical Consideration." In R. M. Smith, G. F. Aker, and J. R. Kidd (Eds.), *Handbook of Adult Education.* New York: Macmillan, 1970.

Craig L. Scanlan is associate professor and chairman of the Department of Health Education, Evaluation, and Research in the School of Health-Related Professions at the University of Medicine and Dentistry of New Jersey, Newark, and assistant director of the graduate program in allied health education for the Graduate School of Education at Rutgers University, New Brunswick, New Jersey.

Continuing educators hold diverse viewpoints on their relationships with the professions. Constructive dialogue on the values and beliefs underlying these viewpoints and their impact on the practice of continuing professional education needs to begin.

Examining the Relationships Between Continuing Educators and the Professions

Ronald M. Cervero, Dieter Bussigel, Mickey Hellyer

Continuing education has become increasingly recognized as having a central role in the education of professionals. It was once seen as a peripheral addition to the centerpiece of professional preparation, preservice education. Now, leaders of many professional groups see continuing professional education as a necessary part of a lifelong educational process. The growth of mandatory continuing education requirements for relicensure and recertification described in Chapter Four is only the most visible symbol of this perspective transformation. Indeed, Houle (1980, p. 302) suggests that what we are witnessing today is a precursor of future events: "What we hardly dare prophesy today will be seen by later generations as efforts to achieve a manifest necessity."

The presumed expertise of continuing educators in needs assessment, program development, and evaluation has allowed them to assume a role in this new movement. Their skills are being accepted both by professional groups and by those who provide continuing professional education for these groups. An increasing number of continuing educators are employed

R. M. Cervero, C. L. Scanlan (Eds.). *Problems and Prospects in Continuing Professional Education.* New Directions for Continuing Education, no. 27. San Francisco: Jossey-Bass, September 1985.

in positions that were closed to them in the past, for example, as directors of continuing education in professional associations; previously, only people trained in the profession itself have served in such positions. Many continuing educators believe that this is an extremely positive development because it means that they have been accepted as experts by the most powerful and elite groups in society.

In spite of these developments, criticism of continuing education's involvement with the professions has emerged from within the field. This criticism has forced continuing educators to look beyond their perceived role as supplying format expertise for the development of educational programs and to consider the social function of professionalism in the context of a socially stratified society in which the professions occupy a position of increasing status and power. The AEA/USA Task Force on Voluntary Learning (1980, p. 3) strongly condemned mandatory continuing education for perpetuating "professional autonomy at the expense of consumers." Rockhill (1976, p. 9) thinks that continuing educators have a choice: "We can welcome increased certification requirements as the 'gold rush of '76' and provide mandatory continuing education programs . . . or we can seek ways of overcoming injustices within the system by 1) developing meaningful checks upon professional control and 2) opposing mandatory continuing education." Rockhill presents a case for the second alternative.

Continuing educators hold divergent viewpoints on their appropriate relationship to the professions. Some observers argue that continuing educators are improving society by helping professionals to become more competent. In this view, professions are a positive force within society; by improving their competence as individuals and power as groups, professionals can better serve their clients. In contrast, critics claim that continuing professional educators are making society more unequal by contributing to the growth of the professional caste system. This view holds that the professions as currently conceived are a negative force within society and that anything that enhances their image, mystique, monopoly, and power is in the long run harmful to those segments of society that are less powerful.

The debate over continuing professional education originates in differing ideological perspectives on professionalism held by continuing educators and in their differing conceptions of the purposes of education. The intent of this chapter is to clarify and explore these issues within an analytical framework of the divergent ideological viewpoints currently characterizing practice in continuing professional education. For this framework, we have selected two variables that we believe are crucial for understanding the different ideological viewpoints held by continuing educators: the perspective on professionalism and the focus of the educational intervention.

Overview

The framework modeled in Figure 1 categorizes the ideological viewpoints of continuing educators on the relationship of their work to the professions. The framework is a two-dimensional matrix that distinguishes four fundamentally different points of view. The horizontal dimension defines continuing educators' viewpoints regarding the concept of professionalism. These viewpoints are best understood as existing on a continuum whose two end points represent the traditional and revisionist interpretations of professionalism. The vertical dimension represents a continuum of viewpoints regarding continuing educators' stance toward the desired focus of educational intervention. The two endpoints of this continuum are the individual and the social structural level. The term *social structural level* refers to the effect that continuing education may have on phenomena larger than individuals, such as professional groups, or on structural relationships among different classes in society. These dimensions are described in detail in following sections. This analytical framework for the interpretation of the issue is aimed at enhancing our critical self-awareness as continuing educators for the professions. Critical self-awareness is grounded in the link between beliefs, values, and action.

As Chapter One has shown, continuing educators' actions are a direct function of their beliefs. Thus, the framework described here discusses how the actions of continuing educators vary depending on their ideological stance. The framework should be seen as a tool for clarifying ideas, not classifying people. Although we quote individual authors to illustrate particular views, the reader should not assume that an author is best represented by that view. The matrix is intended not to portray clearly delineated categories but to describe the many ideological orientations underlying continuing educators' practice.

The Focus of Educational Intervention Dimension

The focus of education intervention dimension has been defined most clearly by Heaney (1983, p. 1): "Most education can be categorized in one or two ways: Either it aims to enhance personal growth and the perfection of individual potentials, or it seeks to coordinate and unify individual initiatives so that, through collective action, the capacities of a group are increased." Of course, continuing educators at both ends of the continuum work with individuals. The viewpoint that identifies the individual as the appropriate focus for educational intervention—a psychologically oriented perspective—assumes that social structure necessarily improves when individuals' consciousness is enhanced and their competence and performance are improved. The social structural focus—a soci-

**Figure 1. Ideological Viewpoints on the Relationship Between
Continuing Educators and the Professions**

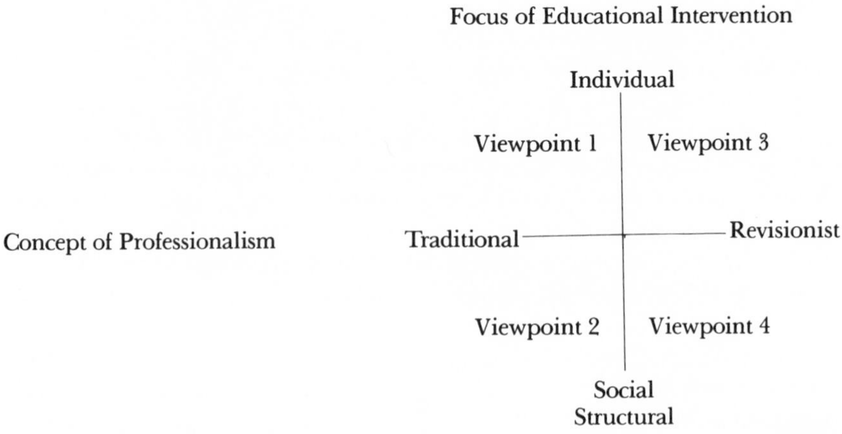

Focus of Educational Intervention

Individual

	Viewpoint 1	Viewpoint 3

Concept of Professionalism   Traditional ——————————— Revisionist

	Viewpoint 2	Viewpoint 4

Social
Structural

ologically oriented perspective—sees individuals not as the end of educative efforts but as the means to achieve social and structural improvements. Thus, those at the two ends of the continuum differ in what they consider the focus of their educational interventions: individual change or social and structural change.

The individual focus in continuing professional education is exemplified by Cruse's (1983, pp. 45–46) description of the learning needs of certified public accountants: "Because the developmental needs of CPAs are individual, each CPA should be responsible for his or her own professional development. He or she is in the best position, with guidance from the firm or employer, to assess his or her own learning needs and identify the precise continuing professional education programs to serve those needs when they exist." The role of continuing educators in this scheme is to help CPAs define their learning needs and to provide programs that meet those needs.

This focus on individual needs has been criticized for ignoring the broader consequences of continuing education: "In individual terms, practitioners observe real 'growth' in their participants. People gain new information, develop new skills, competencies, and confidence . . . Thus, at the individual level, the continuing education process appears to be dynamic. Yet, in a wider context, nothing has substantially changed" (Law and Sissons, 1983, p. 2). Houle (1980, p. 306) argues that working with individual needs, such as keeping up to date with new developments in the profession, is too limited a focus for continuing professional education; rather, "the goals of professional education, including those of continuing learn-

ing, should be concerned with the entire process of professionalization."
For Houle, the focus of educational intervention is primarily the social
structural entity of the profession. He envisions continuing professional
education as contributing directly to the professionalization process of
occupations.

The Viewpoint on Professionalism Dimension

The concept of professionalism has undergone a dramatic transformation since mid century. At that time, a clear distinction was drawn
between professions and other occupational groups, and the latter were
seen as legitimately striving to become the former. In Figure 1, this is
called the traditional perspective. In recent years, some sociologists and
historians have suggested a radically different perspective; in Figure 1, it
is called the revisionist perspective. Revisionists are inclined to view the
professions as occupations that seek power and influence in the political
arena and the marketplace. Continuing educators' viewpoints toward the
professions fall somewhere between the two ends of the continuum.

The traditional approach tends to emphasize certain special characteristics that an occupation has to attain in order to call itself a profession. George Ritzer (1977) has summarized six characteristics that
differentiate professions from other occupations. In general, says Ritzer, the
traditionalist literature characterizes a profession as any occupation that
has attained all the following:

- General systematic knowledge that is its exclusive possession
- A norm of autonomy that the law and the public are bound to respect
- A norm of altruism that entitles the profession to special treat-
  ment and respect
- A norm of authority over clients that the public feels is its duty
  to obey
- A distinctive occupational culture
- Recognition by the community and the law that the occupation
  is a profession.

Let us take the first characteristic as our example. Traditionalists
argue that the professions possess a unique and formal knowledge base.
Furthermore, they contend that this knowledge can be conveyed only
within the structured environment of a formal training program or by
means of the informal exchange between a member of the profession and
the aspiring student. Ernest Greenwood (1957, p. 46) sums up this position
quite well: "The crucial distinction between profession and nonprofession
is that the skills which characterize a profession flow from and are supported by a fund of knowledge that has been organized into an internally
consistent system called a body of theory."

While traditionalists argue that certain traits distinguish the professions from other occupations, the revisionist perspective emphasizes the idea that "a profession may not really possess [all these] traits: It may simply have the power to convince the public, law, and so forth that it possess[es] them" (Ritzer, 1977, p. 56). Johnson (1972, p. 45) presents the fundamental starting point for the revisionist point of view: "Professionalism, then, becomes redefined as a peculiar type of occupational control rather than an expression of the inherent nature of particular occupations. A profession is not, then, an occupation but a means of controlling an occupation."

For Johnson, the characteristics that distinguish a profession for traditionalists are not definitions of occupations but rather "the characteristics of a peculiar form of occupational control" (p. 27). Thus, professions are seen as groups of individuals seeking to improve their occupational and economic status. The most potent strategic weapon that these groups use in their conflict with other groups in society is the ideology of professionalism.

Four Viewpoints on the Relationship Between Continuing Educators and the Professions

Viewpoint 1: Individual, Traditional. Several ideas characterize the first viewpoint, which we can characterize as the individual, traditional viewpoint. Continuing educators are capable of making decisions only about the format and structure of educational activities. Firmly planted in the traditional perspective is the view that an occupation either is or is not a profession and that continuing education cannot change this basic categorization. In this stance, the ultimate goal of continuing educators is to help professionals provide higher-quality service to clients by improving their competence, their performance, or both. Prototypical continuing educators realize that occupations control their own professionalization process, accept their subservient role of helping professionals to make decisions about the design (not the content) of their educational activities, and strive to become skilled at making programming decisions about continuing professional education.

This stance, perhaps the most prevalent of the four, is defined in the literature more by what authors omit than by what they include in their overall models of continuing education. That is, many authors who provide overall systems or conceptions of continuing professional education do not address directly the relationship between continuing educators and the professions. Examples include LeBreton and Associates (1979) and Lauffer (1977). In describing an overall system for the continuing education of professionals, LeBreton and Associates identify five subsystems: need opportunity awareness, need assessment, program development, implementation, and postimplementation. Their discussion implies that the relationship of the continuing educator to the professional group is at the level of individual members, not at the social structural level of the profession. While the details of this viewpoint vary from one author to another, the following passage from LeBreton and Associates (1979, p. 8) typifies the technological dimensions of responsibility: "Increasingly, one needs a planned approach to professional development if one's professional competence is to be maintained and enlarged. Continuing education specialists play a major facilitating role in this endeavor. They may assist in the determination of developmental needs of clients, design programs in view of expressed needs, and arrange for their implementation."

In his models of practice framework, Lauffer (1977) describes the consumers of continuing professional education as individual learners or the service agency, not the occupation as a whole. Like LeBreton and Associates, Lauffer undertakes to identify the problems that these consumers have and to "treat" them through well-planned continuing education. There is no sense that the problems to which continuing professional education is the solution are derived from the profession as a whole, that is, from the collective interests of the group. The final characteristic of this viewpoint, the subservience of continuing educators to professional groups, is illustrated by Lauffer (1977, p. 195): "It is insufficient for continuing educators to claim a separate occupation or the mandate to perform certain functions. Both mandate and authority must be conferred by outside institutions, such as regulating groups, employing agencies, professional associations, and individual consumers."

Viewpoint 2: Social Structural, Traditional. The second viewpoint differs from the first in that educational intervention focuses on the social structural level of the entire profession. However, like viewpoint 1, viewpoint 2 accepts the traditional conception of professionalism. Examples of these ideas can be found in Houle (1980).

Although Houle rejects the notion that there is a charmed circle of professions distinct from other occupations, he still believes that professionalism is an ideal worth achieving. Houle (1980, pp. 26–27) explains that his view "calls for a new use of the criteria long associated with the professions. Each criterion sets a standard that may be considered either in static or dynamic terms. In the past, the major search has been for absolutes that would identify those occupations that could properly be called professions. The more widespread modern trend is to ask what principles of action seem most significant to the members of a vocation as they seek to elevate and dignify its work so that it can become accepted by society as a profession."

Continuing education, in Houle's view, is intimately intertwined with this dynamic process of professionalization: "The dynamic concept of professionalism requires the broadening of the present goals of continuing education. Many leaders assume that the dominant (perhaps exclusive) objectives of such learning are the mastery of new theoretical and practical knowledge. . . . But, the professionalizing process is complex, and the life-long learning to which it gives rise must have many goals. . . . Fourteen characteristics broadly associated with the professionalization process are here suggested as bases for such goals" (Houle, 1980, p. 34). Thus, Houle's basic premise is that continuing education should be used to aid the professionalization process.

From this viewpoint, the prototypical continuing educator is one who accepts the ideal of professionalization and works as a full partner with professionalizing vocations in seeking this ideal. Houle (1980, pp. 30-31) argues that "a dynamic concept of professionalization offers educators both the opportunity and the challenge to use active principles of learning to help achieve the basic aims of the group with which they work. They become not merely reinforcers of the status quo, as they so often are now, but the colleagues of all who work to further the power and the responsibility of the vocation. They serve but are not subservient."

Continuing educators should conceive of themselves not as subservient actors in the professionalizing process, responsible only for design decisions. Rather, they should be equal partners concerned with the entire process of professionalization, and they should be responsible for the contribution that continuing education can make to this process.

Viewpoint 3: Individual, Revisionist. Like viewpoint 1, viewpoint 3 focuses on the individual. Yet, because continuing educators who take this viewpoint accept the revisionist understanding of professionalism, the learning needs that they see are entirely different from the needs identified from viewpoint 1. The revisionists see a need for a fundamental shift of power, which is held primarily by professionals, in the relationship between professional and client. A central belief is that both professionals and clients should be educated to accept a more equal relationship between the two. The continuing educator who holds this viewpoint believes that professions are elitist social groups whose knowledge and power must be shared with clients and that the way of achieving the needed fundamental shift in the conception of professionalism is by changing the attitudes of individuals, professionals, and clients through education.

A central characteristic of the revisionist viewpoint is that professional groups control knowledge for the purpose of maintaining power, controlling the market for their services, and achieving economic gain. Illich (1977, p. 15) describes this view of profession: "Let us first face the fact that the bodies of specialists that now dominate the creation, adjudication, and implementation of needs are a new kind of cartel. They are more deeply entrenched than a Byzantine bureaucracy, more international than a world church, more stable than any labor union . . . and equipped with a tighter hold over those they claim as victims than any mafia."

Continuing educators should seek to change the situation that Illich describes by changing the way in which individuals understand professionalism. This line of reasoning assumes that, if enough individuals change their behavior, then the existing system of professionalism will change. Woll (1984, p. 175) writes: "If what . . . continuing education as a field has to offer the professionalizing vocations is not about vision, new ways of thought . . . then it is a hollow, empty enterprise that should be abandoned. And, if it is about critical thought and vision, then it must cherish the place where thought and vision take place, inside each individual human being, where the interactions . . . we have with one another and the world are registered and take on meaning."

Continuing educators in this cell are concerned not about improving professionals' performance but rather about changing their attitudes and their conceptions of the world. They believe that, if professionals and consumers alike become more critical of the current problems posed by a ruling professional caste, then a more equitable distribution of knowledge, power, and service will follow.

Viewpoint 4: Social Structural, Revisionist. The fourth viewpoint shares two things with the third: the revisionist understanding of professionalism and the desire to redress the balance of power between professionals, who represent the elite class of society, and those who suffer from a disadvantaged position in the class structure. This viewpoint differs from viewpoint 3 in that it sees the problem as located in the sociopolitical structure of groups within society, not in the minds of individuals. Thus, the focus of educational interventions must be at the social structural, not the individual, level. The form that the resulting interventions take has been termed *community activism, community organizing,* and *liberatory education.* The prototypical continuing educator in this viewpoint views professionals as engaged in a class struggle with oppressed members of society. These educators work with the oppressed groups and, through their educational efforts, seek to improve their chances for success. Thus, in this view continuing educators work with professions in the same way that Ralph Nader can be understood as having worked with the auto industry, that is, in an adversarial role. While this viewpoint is similar to viewpoint 2 in its emphasis on the focusing of educational efforts at the social structural level, it differs dramatically in its identification of the problem.

Heaney (1984, pp. 117–118) provides insight into a central characteristic of this viewpoint: "Social systems and technologies are not neutral; they can limit freedom in ways that are not directly subject to human volition. Opponents of racism and sexism correctly direct their energies toward systemic rather than attitudinal change. . . . Systems can operate independently of the persons who appear to guide them. In such cases, it is more important to change the system than to influence the bosses." Thus, the attitudes and competence of professionals are not the problem to which solutions should be addressed. Rather, the problem lies in the oppressive system of which professionals are a part. Working with individual professionals is the least effective way of solving the problems defined by the majority of those whose views are consistent with this perspective. However, there are small subgroups in many professions that work collectively to change the fundamental relationship between their profession and society. For example, there are physicians who work to make the provision of health care equitable, and there are teachers who work to change the role that schools play in the reproduction of existing social relations. Continuing educators who work with these subgroups, like the majority of those in this cell, also seek to change the system, albeit by different means from those of the majority.

Conclusion

This chapter has analyzed the ways in which continuing educators think about the relationship between their work and the professions. We recognize that no analytical framework used to separate conceptions of reality represents viewpoints in their full richness and complexity. We hope that continuing educators are willing to accept this limitation so that the issues can be brought into sharper focus.

We believe that the normative dimensions of the issues represent the primary focus of the debate among continuing educators; that is, the debate should focus on what the relationship between continuing educators and the professions should be. Because the issues involve fundamental values and assumptions that continuing educators hold about the characteristics of a good society and the best means of achieving such a society, it is unreasonable to expect that consensus is possible. Nevertheless, we believe that continuing educators, individually and collectively, should examine critically the relationship of their work to the professions. Critical analysis should prove useful in helping continuing educators to grasp the purpose of their endeavors, and ultimately it should help continuing professional education to articulate its role and functions to society at large.

References

Adult Education Association of the U.S.A. Task Force on Voluntary Learning. *Task Force Report.* Washington, D.C.: AAACE, 1980.
Cruse, R. B. "The Accounting Profession." In M. R. Stern (Ed.), *Power and Conflict in Continuing Professional Education.* Belmont, Calif.: Wadsworth, 1983.
Greenwood, E. "Attributes of a Profession." *Social Work,* 1957, 2, 46–52.
Heaney, T. W. "Individual and Social Reconstruction: Confrontation or Dialectic." Paper presented at the meeting of the Commission of Professors of Adult Education, Philadelphia, November 29, 1983.
Heaney, T. W. "Action, Freedom, and Liberatory Education." In S. B. Merriam

(Ed.), *Selected Writings on Philosophy and Adult Education*. Malabar, Fla.: Krieger, 1984.

Houle, C. O. *Continuing Learning in the Professions*. San Francisco: Jossey-Bass, 1980.

Illich, I. *Disabling Professions*. London: Marion Boyars, 1977.

Johnson, T. J. *Professions and Power*. London: Macmillan, 1972.

Lauffer, A. *The Practice of Continuing Education in the Human Services*. New York: McGraw-Hill, 1977.

Law, M., and Sissons, L. "Ideology and Needs in Continuing Education." Paper presented at a conference of the New Zealand Association for Research in Education, Wellington, December 9, 1983.

LeBreton, P. P., and Associates (Eds.). *The Evaluation of Continuing Education for Professionals: A Systems View*. Seattle: University of Washington, 1979.

Ritzer, G. *Working, Conflict, and Change*. Englewood Cliffs, N.J.: Prentice-Hall, 1977.

Rockhill, K. "The Mystique of Certification, Education, and Professionalism: In Service of Whom?" In J. S. Long and R. Boshier (Eds.), *Certification, Credentialing, Licensing, and the Renewal Process*. Moscow, Ind.: News Review Publishing, 1976.

Woll, B. "The Empty Ideal: A Critique of *Continuing Learning in the Professions* by Cyril O. Houle." *Adult Education Quarterly*, 1984, *34*, 167–177.

Ronald M. Cervero is associate professor of adult and continuing education in the Department of Leadership and Educational Policy Studies at Northern Illinois University, DeKalb.

Dieter Bussigel and Mickey Hellyer are doctoral candidates in the adult and continuing education program at Northern Illinois University.

Recent developments in the study of professionals'
reasons for participation in continuing professional
education have important implications for
practitioners, policy makers, and scholars.

Assessing Professionals' Reasons for Participating in Continuing Education

Arden D. Grotelueschen

An important and underdeveloped area of knowledge concerns professionals' reasons for participating in continuing education activities. This chapter reviews and critically analyzes the literature on educational participation
and focuses on the special case of continuing professional education by
presenting an alternative to traditional approaches to understanding participation in continuing education. Findings resulting from this approach
are described, and the implications of this new knowledge are discussed.

Why Adults Participate in Education

Together with adult learning, instruction, and program planning,
educational participation is one of the central concepts in the study of
continuing education (Rubenson, 1982). In this chapter, educational participation is understood to include involvement in formal educational
activities for professionals that are typically short-term, part-time, or both.
The providers of such activities include educational institutions, professional associations and societies, professional service agencies, the government, and other organizations with clearly recognized responsibilities for
providing educational programs for professionals.

R. M. Cervero, C. L. Scanlan (Eds.). *Problems and Prospects in Continuing Professional Education.* New Directions
for Continuing Education, no. 27. San Francisco: Jossey-Bass, September 1985.

Because continuing education is generally voluntary, it has been important for educators to understand the reasons for adults' participation in educational activities. The literature on reasons for participation has been analyzed in terms both of models of participation that have emerged from the research (Cross, 1981) and of conceptualizations that have been used to guide inquiry on participation in continuing education (Douglah, 1970). Most of these models are grounded in psychology. They treat participation as an end and conceptualize reasons for participation as antecedent conditions. For the most part, their reasons for participation have been deduced from psychological or sociopsychological theory, and their results do not necessarily focus on either the felt reasons of participants themselves or on the practical implications of research findings for continuing education practice.

One notable exception to such psychologically oriented and theory-based models is the typology of adult learning orientations advanced by Houle (1961). Beginning with participants' reasons for participation, Houle described a typology of learning orientations that included activity-oriented, learning-oriented, and goal-oriented participants. Research has attempted to validate Houle's learning orientations by using three separate instruments: the Continuing Learning Orientation Index (Sheffield, 1964), the Reasons for Participation Instrument, (Burgess, 1971; Grabowski, 1972), and the Education Participation Scale (Boshier, 1971; Boshier and Collins, 1982; Morstain and Smart, 1974).

While these studies have helped us to understand why adults participate in continuing education, their theoretical emphasis has generally overshadowed the need to address ways in which this knowledge can be used to improve practice. Moreover, the tendency to focus on the adult population in general has limited the applicability of research findings, particularly in regard to highly differentiated subgroups, such as professionals. Many of the items and factors that have emerged from the studies of the adult population in general are of questionable appropriateness as reasons for professionals' participation in continuing education, and consequently they are of doubtful utility for planners and developers of continuing professional education. These limitations suggest that continuing professional education should be treated as a special case and that an alternative approach to the study of professionals' participation is needed.

Continuing Professional Education as a Special Case

It is important to make a distinction between continuing education in general and continuing professional education in particular. The specialized status of continuing professional education affects how we conceptualize, study, and practice it. This contention is based on observations in three areas: the characteristics of the referent population, the nature of participation, and the educational beneficiaries of continuing professional education. Each area has implications for research and practice.

Characteristics of the Referent Population. The referent population of continuing professional education is a group of adult learners who are categorized by their occupational status and by their participation in continuing education activities. Thus, as a group the target population is more homogeneous than the universe of adults in general. While this homogeneity is only relative, applying perhaps more to such traditional professional occupations as medicine, law, dentistry, nursing, and pharmacy, it is reasonable to suggest that it increasingly applies to occupational groups with emerging professional status, such as allied health, business, education, and social work.

While the characteristics of these specific occupations do vary (Grotelueschen and others, 1981a, 1981b), when considered as a whole they resist some traditionally key discriminating variables in continuing education research. As already noted, the most prominent of these variables is the participant's level of formal education (Anderson and Darkenwald, 1979). Long held to be one of the strongest predictors of participation in continuing education, level of formal education operates primarily as a constant within most professional groups. Another important variable has been occupational status, which also shows relatively little variability among professional groups when they are compared with the adult education population in general.

The recognition that continuing education and continuing professional education have significantly different referent populations has both theoretical and practical implications. First, the conceptual orientation of theory and research in general continuing education may be inadequate or inappropriate for continuing professional education. Second, the findings from continuing education research on participation may not be generalizable to continuing professional education, and it may therefore not be very useful for guiding its practice.

The Nature of Participation. Another issue that carries implications for research concerns the decision-making autonomy of participants in continuing professional education. Whereas general adult learners are often characterized as volunteers for learning, professionals may have somewhat less choice. Professionals are often expected to participate as a result of relicensure requirements of intraprofessional norms, yet time, cost, and the availability of relevant programming pose significant constraints (Scanlan and Darkenwald, 1984). This state of affairs represents a general erosion of decision-making autonomy on the part of professionals regarding educational participation. Not only is the decision to participate often predetermined, but so, too, are the professional's decisions about where and when to participate.

These factors challenge continuing professional educators to provide the best educational services possible (Houle, 1980). The challenge is intensified by the contemporary economic climate and by the concurrent interest in providing as much high-quality local programming as possible. This observation carries the pragmatic implication that research on continuing professional education should be designed so that it can assist and guide practitioners in providing responsive, high-quality educational programming. To the extent that existing research in general continuing education fails to do this, it would be useful to treat research on continuing professional education as a special case.

The Educational Beneficiaries. The third area of consideration is the identification of educational beneficiaries. In continuing education in general as well as in continuing professional education, learners are generally seen as both participants in and beneficiaries of education. However, as Chapters One and Two have shown, there is a strong predisposition among the providers of continuing professional education to regard as beneficiaries persons or groups once removed from the educational activity (for example, patients, clients, insurance companies, and those concerned with the public health and welfare). It is sometimes even argued that continuing professional education is successful only when benefits accrue to such secondary beneficiaries (Houle, 1980).

This broad perspective (discussed by Kenny in the next chapter) is supported by policies that promote and sustain mandatory continuing professional education. Such policies assume that secondary beneficiaries—consumers of professional services, professional associations, institutional providers of services, regulatory agencies, and the public in general—all have a vested interest in continuing professional education. The benefits that secondary targets receive can be improved health care, better public image, more proficient personnel, increased ability to monitor licensed professionals, and more efficient administration of public services. These benefits and beneficiaries are often the raison d'être for continuing professional education. While continuing professional educators can not be held entirely accountable for benefits once or twice removed, it is their responsibility to address them as best they can.

An Alternative Approach

During the past decade, several members of the Office of the Study of Continuing Professional Education at the University of Illinois at Urbana-Champaign have been involved in developmental research on professionals' reasons for participation in continuing professional education. As a result of this effort, an extensive data bank has been established, and a variety of instruments have been developed. The Participation Reasons Scale (PRS) (Grotelueschen and others, 1979b; Kenny and Harnisch, 1982) has been central to this research. The PRS has been administered to random samples of professionals at state, regional, and national levels as well as to a few local population groups. Findings from these studies have been presented at national professional meetings (Grotelueschen and others, 1979c, 1980, 1981a; Catlin and Anderson, 1982), reported in dissertations and unpublished reports (Catlin, 1928b; Groteleuschen and others, 1979a; Grotelueschen and Harnisch, 1978-1981; Harnisch, 1980; Macrina, 1982), and published in the professional literature (Catlin, 1982a; Cervero, 1981; Kenny and Harnisch, 1982). This section introduces this alternative line of research on participation. It pays special attention to the goals, developmental history, and technical aspects of the PRS.

Assumptions. This line of research is based on three assumptions. The first is that professionals' participation in continuing professional education is a purposeful activity. That is, it is assumed that participation in continuing education should yield outcomes relevant to professional practice, regardless of what caused participation. It is our interest, therefore, to treat participation as a means and to attend to the issue of what it can bring about, such as remediation, growth, and change, rather than to what brought it about, such as peer pressure, mandation, and so on. We do not deny that such forces may have an effect on participation, we are more interested in what continuing educators can do to help bring about educationally relevant outcomes.

Our second assumption is that the reasons for participation should have a fundamentally educational focus. Reasons for participation should be oriented to achieving an educational goal and be relevant for educational program developers. For example, escaping from routine is not a good reason for participation. It does not say why educational participation would be especially relevant, neither does it suggest much that a continuing educator could do in response to that need. This focus is intended not to downplay the importance of other reasons for participation, such as therapeutic goals or psychological antecedents, but to address the practice domain of the continuing educator as educator, not as counselor, psychiatrist, or entertainer.

Our third assumption addresses the concern over what constitutes goals or educational outcomes relevant to professional practice. Like Scanlan in Chapter One, we recognize that continuing professional education has both traditional and explicit purposes and less traditional purposes that respond to the demands of the professional role in modern society. Reasons included in the basic PRS instrument cluster into dimensions that respond to both traditional and nontraditional purposes of continuing professional education. The more traditional clusters of reasons are related to professional development and improvement as well as to the quality of professional service. The less traditional clusters of reasons are related to personal benefits and job security, collegial learning and interaction, and reflection on and commitment to the state of one's profession and one's relationship to it.

The Participation Reasons Scale. The PRS is a self-report instrument. It states educational reasons for participating in continuing professional education. The statements are specific to a given profession. The respondent's task is to indicate on a seven-point Likert-type scale the relative importance of the reasons for participation in a specific continuing education activity or in continuing education in general. One represents not important, while seven represents extremely important.

The instrument has been refined as data have been gathered and analyzed. The various forms differ in the number of items and in their applicability to a specific profession. The nineteen-item PRS–19 was the first to be developed; it was for business professionals, orthopedic surgeons, and veterinarians. It evolved into the thirty-five-statement PRS–35, which was applied to business professionals, nurses, social workers, physicians, and veterinarians. The most recent form is the thirty-statement PRS–30, which has been applied to business professionals, judges, physicians, public health administrators, hospital administrators, pharmacists, and dentists (Figure 1). The evolution from nineteen, to thirty-five, to thirty statements reflects the concern for maximizing the reliability and validity of the PRS for specific professions while keeping it short.

The reliability of the PRS is measured by the internal consistency of the clusters of reasons (factors) that emerge when responses from particular professional groups are analyzed. Administration of the PRS to veterinarians (Harnisch, 1980), judges (Catlin, 1982a, 1982b), and public health administrators (Macrina, 1982) confirms that the PRS factor scales exhibit satisfactory levels of reliability, with coefficients ranging from a low of .78 to a high of .92.

The PRS has undergone both content and face validation. Content validation was an integral component of the development process. Item generation was based on analysis of the literature on participation and survey of representatives of selected professional groups. Once constructed, a sample of continuing educators rated the prototype PRS for appropriateness as a measure of professionals' reasons for participation. Consistently high ratings of appropriateness provided additional evidence of the scale's validity. Recent findings across several professional groups tend to substantiate these early efforts to assure that the PRS is measuring what it intends to measure (Harnisch, 1980; Catlin, 1982a, 1982b; Cervero, 1981; Grotelueschen and others, 1979a; Macrina, 1982).

Auxiliary Instruments. The PRS has been designed for use alone and with other instruments and in a variety of situations and for a variety of purposes. The PRS can be used to assess professionals' reasons for participation in continuing professional education in general by administering

Figure 1. Facsimile of Physician Participation Reason Scale

Directions: There are many reasons for participation in continuing professional education activities. The following items are designed so that you can indicate the relative importance of the general reasons you might have for participating in this specific continuing medical education activity. For each item, mark the numeral which best represents the degree of importance you attach to each reason.

Reasons	Not Important		Moderately Important			Very Important	
1. To further match my knowledge or skills with the demands of my medical activities	1	2	3	4	5	6	7
2. To mutually exchange thoughts with medical colleagues	1	2	3	4	5	6	7
3. To help me be more productive in my professional role	1	2	3	4	5	6	7
4. To enable me to better meet patient expectations	1	2	3	4	5	6	7
5. To maintain my current abilities	1	2	3	4	5	6	7
6. To increase the likelihood of benefits for family and friends	1	2	3	4	5	6	7
7. To relate my ideas to those of my professional peers	1	2	3	4	5	6	7
8. To maintain my identity with my profession	1	2	3	4	5	6	7
9. To accommodate more effectively to the needs of my patients	1	2	3	4	5	6	7
10. To review my commitment to my profession	1	2	3	4	5	6	7
11. To increase the likelihood of personal financial gain	1	2	3	4	5	6	7
12. To learn from the interaction with other physicians	1	2	3	4	5	6	7
13. To help me develop leadership capabilities for my profession	1	2	3	4	5	6	7
14. To increase my proficiency with patients	1	2	3	4	5	6	7
15. To consider changing the emphasis of my present medical responsibilities	1	2	3	4'	5	6	7
16. To develop new professional knowledge and skills	1	2	3	4	5	6	7
17. To sharpen my perspective of my professional role or practice	1	2	3	4	5	6	7
18. To help me keep abreast of new developments in medicine	1	2	3	4	5	6	7
19. To help me increase the likelihood that patients are better served	1	2	3	4	5	6	7
20. To assess the direction in which my profession is going	1	2	3	4	5	6	7
21. To help me be more competent in my medical work	1	2	3	4	5	6	7
22. To increase the likelihood of professional advancement	1	2	3	4	5	6	7
23. To be challenged by the thinking of my medical colleagues	1	2	3	4	5	6	7
24. To enhance the image of my profession	1	2	3	4	5	6	7
25. To improve my individual service to the public as a physician	1	2	3	4	5	6	7
26. To consider the limitations of my role as a physician	1	2	3	4	5	6	7
27. To develop proficiencies necessary to maintain quality performance	1	2	3	4	5	6	7
28. To enhance my individual security in my present medical position	1	2	3	4	5	6	7
29. To maintain the quality of my medical service	1	2	3	4	5	6	7
30. To reflect on the value of my medical responsibilities	1	2	3	4	5	6	7

Source: Published Scale © 1980 by Evaluation and Development Services Co.

it to samples of professionals who are not presently attending a specific educational activity. It can also be used to assess professionals' reasons for participation in a particular program by administering it at the program. The former use yields data relevant to theory development. The latter use yields data relevant to formative and summative evaluation.

The PRS was designed to be administered in conjunction with a Respondent Information Form (RIF). The RIF collects demographic data of two basic types. First, it collects data on demographic dimensions common to all professionals, including such person-related variables as sex, income level, and age. These data are useful for developing theory applicable to all professionals and for developing basic descriptive data on demographic dimensions that are specific to the profession, including such profession-related variables as years in practice, practice setting, type of practice, and area of specialization. These data are useful for developing theory and for providing specific data for program development within a particular profession (Harnisch, 1980).

By converting the items into the past tense, we have modified the PRS to yield the Participation Benefits Scale (PBS). In the context of specific programs, the PBS can be used as a posttest form of the PRS to provide data useful for program evaluation and educational accountability (Grotelueschen and Harnisch, 1978-1981). The PBS can be used with random samples to assess professionals' perception of the overall impact of participation in continuing professional education. As such, it can yield data of importance for policy analysts and policy makers.

Utility of the Findings

Administration of the PRS and its auxiliary instruments to a variety of professional groups has provided information useful to both the continuing education practitioner and the scholar. This knowledge can be grouped into three major areas: One area identifies the different reasons for participation and the differences among reasons both within a profession and across professions. The second area identifies relationships between profession-related characteristics (for example, type of practice, type and setting of employment) and reasons for participation. The third area identifies relationships between person-related characteristics (for example, sex, years in practice) and reasons for participation. Each developing area of knowledge has important implications for practitioners intent on improving their program development, marketing, and evaluation skills as well as for scholars interested in increasing their understanding of the educational development of professionals.

Reasons for Participation. The PRS taps five basic clusters of reasons for participation in continuing professional education: (a) professional improvement and development, (b) professional service, (c) collegial learning and interaction, (d) professional commitment and reflection, and (e) personal benefits and job security. Items administered to physicians that examplify these clusters include the following, respectively: "To maintain my current abilities" (a), "To help me increase the likelihood that patients are better served" (b), "To be challenged by the thinking of my medical colleagues" (c), "To maintain my identity with my profession" (d), and "To enhance my individual security in my present medical profession" (e).

Knowing that the instrument measures these different reasons is important to the continuing educator. For example, it helps to identify program priorities and procedures. If professional improvement and development are high-priority reasons for participation, then professionals are likely to want concrete suggestions that relate to their type of practice. Also, if collegial learning and interaction are highly valued reasons for participation, then it seems likely that the program design should allow for collegial interaction activities. By implication, one can assume that, if participants' expectations are not substantially met, participation in future programs may be negatively affected.

Differences in Reasons for Participation. PRS findings have demonstrated that reasons for professionals' participation in continuing professional education can differ significantly according to the type of profession, the career stage of the professional, the profession-related characteristics of participants, and the person-related characteristics of participants.

Differences According to Profession. Studies conducted among veterinarians, judges, physicians, business professionals, nurses, dentists, social workers, pharmacists, and health educators suggest that, across professions, professional improvement and development items represent the most important cluster of reasons for participation, followed, in order of relative magnitude, by professional service, collegial learning and interaction, professional commitment and reflection, and personal benefits and job security.

The degree of importance attached to each reason cluster differs significantly for individual professions. For example, nurses and social workers rate the improvement and development and services clusters significantly higher than physicians and business executives do. Also, there are significant interaction differences between age and professional groups for a participation reason. For example, there appear to be different rating patterns for the personal benefits and job security cluster between nurses and business professionals on the one hand and judges and physicians on the other. Nurses and business professionals rated these participation reasons higher than judges and physicians, but younger judges and physicians attributed a higher level of importance to this cluster, and younger nurses and business professionals attributed a lower level to it than their older colleagues did.

Differences Within Professions. The relative importance of reasons for participation in continuing professional education also varies within professions. This variation may be due to profession differences or to specific characteristics associated with professionals within the profession. For example, corporate executive business professions give service the lowest rating for participation and collegial learning and interaction one of the highest ratings. Finance business professionals reverse these ratings. They rate service among the highest and collegial learning and interaction among the lowest orientations for participation. These within-profession differences make greater sense if one understands the work and role responsibilities of each of these specific professional groups.

It is also clear that priority shifts within a profession. The shifts are associated with person- and profession-related characteristics. These will be discussed in detail in the next two sections. Here, they are cited to emphasize within-profession differences. For several professional groups (for example, physicians, veterinarians), there is a negative relationship between the number of years of practice and a service orientation to participation.

Person-Related Differences. Profession-related characteristics include such variables as type of practice setting, type of practice, professional membership, and years performing current duties. In general, reasons for participation in continuing professional education relate most strongly to profession-related characteristics. The two orientations that are best explained by profession-related variables are professional improvement and development and professional service. Take, for instance, practice setting and its influence on a professional's reasons for participation. Veterinarians whose principal setting of employment is either the animal clinic or the farm have significantly higher scores on the service cluster than agency veterinarians do. Likewise, pharmacists in hospital settings have a greater orientation to patient service than nonhospital pharmacists do. Physicians in government hospital settings are more oriented to personal benefits and job security and professional reflection and commitment than physicians in proprietary or voluntary hospital settings.

Implications. Findings from applications of the PRS have several implications for practitioners and scholars. First, the most common focus of continuing professional education programming, professional improvement and development, is only one of many reasons why professionals participate in continuing education. Second, professionals differ in the importance that they ascribe to these reasons for participation, both across and within disciplines. Third, differences in reasons for participation within disciplines suggest that professionals undergo a developmental evolution in regard to educational expectations. Fourth, differences in reasons for participation across disciplines suggest that educational expectations vary with characteristics specific to individual professions.

For practitioners, it is clear that a knowledge of their professional clientele's reasons for participation can provide useful guidance in the planning, implementing, and evaluating of continuing professional education programs. Sound planning requires the content and format to correspond to the expectations of those targeted for learning. Once content and format have been chosen, it is most appropriate to market the program to those for whom it has been designed. Likewise, program implementation can logically be based on knowledge of participants' reasons for attending, as can evaluation of the extent to which the effort has met participants' expectations. Moreover, when there are substantial variations in a targeted group's reasons for participation, the opportunity exists to segment the market and provide differential programming or mixed formats that attend to the expectations of varied participants.

For scholars studying the phenomenon of participation, it is becoming increasingly apparent that professionals' expectations regarding continuing professional education are integrally related both to their work and to the modern dynamics of their career lines. The consistency of these findings with Houle's (1980) assumptions regarding the educational development of professionals provides fruitful new grounds for focused inquiry on participation in continuing professional education.

Conclusion

Generally, then, the PRS and the line of research that it supports make a variety of contributions to our knowledge of continuing professional education. While we are still a long way from developing a goal-oriented theory of participation in continuing professional education, we are making some progress, and as we do the PRS yields valuable information for the practice of continuing professional education.

First, the PRS directly and explicitly addresses professionals by recognizing that continuing professional education is a special and significant type of continuing education. As such, the PRS yields information and knowledge demonstrably relevant to continuing professional education.

Second, in conjunction with the RIF and the PBS, the PRS affords continuing professional educators a simple but effective instrument that can help to design programs and monitor specific program performance. In this way, the PRS contributes evaluative precision to the practice of continuing professional education. When used to gather data from a sample of the members of a certain profession, these instruments can also provide information relevant to educational policy analysis for the professions.

Third, these instruments provide information relevant to enhancing the responsiveness and quality of educational programming for professionals. In this way, the line of research described here can elevate the overall level of sophistication in the practice of continuing professional education and its professionalization as a field.

44

Fourth, this approach promotes the applicability of theory and thereby narrows the gap between research and practice. Treating participation as a means to an end, this approach allows for incremental adjustment of the PRS items by attending to feedback from practical applications (for example, evaluations, policy analyses), thus creating a bridge between the requirements of practice and the development of theory. In short, the PRS provides empirical information from the field that can be used to develop theory while concurrently providing guidance for enlightened practice in continuing professional education.

Finally, the research provides a useful line of inquiry in preparation for future exigencies in continuing professional education involving such issues as increased accountability, certification, increased efficiency, and improved effectiveness. It is also the beginning of a data-gathering effort that will ultimately enable us to make some generalizations about professional educational development during the career span both within and across professions. This approach will allow us to advance our understanding of professional educational development and learning and thereby expand our capacity to deal with continuing professional education in a manner that is educationally responsible, knowledgeable, and increasingly professional.

References

Anderson, R. E., and Darkenwald, G. G. *Participation and Persistence in American Adult Education.* New York: College Entrance Examination Board, 1979.

Boshier, R. "Motivation Orientation of Adult Education Participants: A Factor-Analytic Exploration of Houle's Typology." *Adult Education*, 1971, *21*, 3-24.

Boshier, R., and Collins, J. "Education Participation Scale Factor Structure and Correlates for Twelve Thousand Learners." Paper presented at the Adult Education Research Conference, Lincoln, Neb., 1982.

Boshier, R., and Riddell, G. "Education Participation Scale Factor Structure for Older Adults." *Adult Education*, 1978, *28*, 165-175.

Burgess, P. "Reasons for Adult Participation in Group Educational Activities." *Adult Education*, 1971, *22*, 3-29.

Catlin, D. W. "An Empirical Study of Judges' Reasons for Participation in Continuing Professional Education." *Justice System Journal*, 1982a, *7*, 236-256.

Catlin, D. W. "The Relationship Between Selected Characteristics of Judges and Their Reasons for Participation in Continuing Professional Education." Unpublished doctoral dissertation, Michigan State University, 1982b.

Catlin, D. W., and Anderson, W. A. "Why Judges Choose to Participate in Continuing Professional Education." Paper presented at the annual meeting of the American Educational Research Association, New York, 1982.

Cervero, R. M. "A Factor-Analytic Study of Physicians' Reasons for Participating in Continuing Education." *Journal of Medical Education*, 1981, *56*, 29-34.

Cross, K. P. *Adults As Learners: Increasing Participation and Facilitating Learning.* San Francisco: Jossey-Bass, 1981.

Douglah, M. "Some Perspectives on the Phenomenon of Participation." *Adult Education*, 1970, *20*, 88-98

Grabowski, S. M. "Motivational Factors of Adult Learners in a Directed Self-Study Bachelor's Degree Program." Unpublished doctoral dissertation, Syracuse University, 1972.

Grotelueschen, A. D., and Harnisch, D. L. *Program Evaluation Reports: Executive Development.* Urbana: Office for the Study of Continuing Professional Education, University of Illinois at Urbana-Champaign, 1978-1981.

Grotelueschen, A. D., Harnisch, D. L., and Kenny, W. R. *An Analysis of the Participation Reasons Scale Administered to Business Professionals.* Occasional Paper No. 7. Urbana: Office for the Study of Continuing Professional Education, University of Illinois at Urbana-Champaign, 1979a.

Grotelueschen, A. D., Harnisch, D. L., and Kenny, W. R. *Research on Reasons for Participation in Continuing Professional Education: A Statement of Position and Rationale.* Occasional Paper No. 5. Urbana: Office for the Study of Continuing Professional Education, University of Illinois at Urbana-Champaign, 1979b.

Grotelueschen, A. D., Harnisch, D. L., and Kenny, W. R. "Research on Reasons for Participation in Continuing Professional Education: Theory and Practice." Paper presented at the Adult Education Research Conference, Ann Arbor, Mich., 1979c.

Grotelueschen, A. D., Harnisch, D. L., Kenny, W. R., and Cervero, R. M. "Reasons for Participation in Continuing Professional Education." Paper presented at the annual meeting of the American Educational Research Association, Boston, 1980.

Grotelueschen, A. D., Harnisch, D. L., Kenny, W. R., and Cervero, R. M. "A Comparison of Five Professional Groups on the Participation Reasons Scale." Paper presented at the annual meeting of the American Educational Research Association, Los Angeles, 1981a.

Grotelueschen, A. D., Harnisch, D. L., Kenny, W. R., and Cervero, R. M. "A Comparative Approach to Research on Reasons for Participation in Continuing Professional Education." Paper presented at the Adult Education Research Conference, DeKalb, Ill., 1981b.

Harnisch, D. L. "The Continuing Education Reasons of Veterinarians." Unpublished doctoral dissertation, University of Illinois, 1980.

Houle, C. O. *The Inquiring Mind.* Madison: University of Wisconsin Press, 1961.

Houle, C. O. *Continuing Learning in the Professions.* San Francisco: Jossey-Bass, 1980.

Kenny, W. R., and Harnisch, D. L. "A Developmental Approach to Research and Practice in Adult and Continuing Education." *Adult Education,* 1982, *33,* 29-54.

Macrina, D. M. "Continuing Professional Education Needs and Expectations of Health Educators." Unpublished doctoral dissertation, University of Illinois, 1982.

Morstain, B. R., and Smart, J. C. "Reasons for Participation in Adult Education: A Multivariate Analysis of Group Differences." *Adult Education,* 1974, *24,* 83-89.

Rubenson, K. "Adult Education Research: In Quest of a Map of the Territory." *Adult Education,* 1982, *32,* 57-74.

Scanlan, C. L., and Darkenwald, G. G. "Identifying Deterrents to Participation in Continuing Education." *Adult Education Quarterly,* 1984, *34,* 155-166.

Sheffield, S. B. "The Orientation of Adult Continuing Learners." In D. Solomon (Ed.), *The Continuing Learner.* Chicago: Center for the Study of Liberal Education for Adults, 1964.

Arden D. Grotelueschen is professor of educational psychology at the University of Illinois, Urbana-Champaign. He serves as a program and evaluation consultant to several national professional associations. His recent research has focused on professionals' participation in continuing education, content-free learning assessment, and the structure of professional knowledge.

Planning continuing professional education programs under accreditation standards demands effective management of both educational and informational resources.

Program Planning and Accreditation

W. Robert Kenny

In numerous professions, mechanisms have been developed for quality assurance in continuing education, and they are now being applied. These mechanisms use a formal external review and recognition process known as accreditation to evaluate quality and assess compliance with educational standards. This chapter examines some of the tasks and challenges of planning and developing continuing professional education programs within the context of accreditation. It considers the planner's role from two fundamental and interdependent perspectives: the planner as a manager of information and the planner as a manager of education. It identifies and discusses emerging areas of educational responsibility that provide challenges and leadership opportunities for continuing educators who practice in settings where accreditation is operating.

The Emergence of an Education Industry

During the past three decades, formal continuing education for professionals has proliferated dramatically, leaving few if any professions completely untouched. This growth has been accompanied by increased involvement of many types of organizations in the provision of continuing education activities to professionals. These organizations include profes-

R. M. Cervero, C. L. Scanlan (Eds.). *Problems and Prospects in Continuing Professional Education.* New Directions for Continuing Education, no. 27. San Francisco: Jossey-Bass, September 1985.

sional schools; universities; professional associations at the national, state, regional, and local levels; corporations involved in the manufacture, distribution, and provision of goods and services related to professional practice; institutions that provide or broker professional services; government agencies; advertising firms; and a host of for-profit and not-for-profit educational corporations that range from small businesses operating on a part-time basis to multimillion-dollar enterprises with extensive professional staffs and international offices.

This service industry has emerged in response to the increased educational demands and expectations that have been placed on professionals. The demands and expectations of the general public, lawmakers, regulatory bodies, the press, and professionals themselves have all played a role. These forces can be categorized into two groups: those that are related to licensure and those that are not.

Expectations Related to Licensure. Some of the pressures for the growth in continuing professional education are related to the practice of licensing professionals. Such pressure is most clearly evident in regulations that mandate participation in continuing professional education as a prerequisite for periodic relicensure. The breadth of this expectation is illustrated in Table 1, which summarizes the extent of mandatory continuing professional education in selected professions. The growth of mandatory continuing education indicates that the overall trend toward requiring participation in continuing education as a prerequisite for relicensure continues.

Expectations Unrelated to Licensure. It is not clear how fast mandatory continuing education for relicensure will continue to grow. Thus, perhaps the more significant phenomenon is the parallel growth of participation in continuing professional education as a professional expectation. The spread of such expectation is in part a response to external pressures. In this sense, professions seem to be responding to an emerging consumerism regarding professional services, a consumerism that is reflected in increased public awareness and in a growing understanding of the need for lifelong learning. Educational participation is becoming a fact of professional life in the eyes of the public, the press, and state legislatures; professionals themselves; and competing professional practitioner groups who view continuing professional education as a way of achieving enhanced professional status. That this view is taking hold is evident in several emerging professions, where continuing education is viewed as a profession-developing activity that enhances the image of the occupation by establishing linkages with professional recognition systems, such as certification and fellowship status in specialty societies.

Participation in continuing professional education that is unrelated to licensure may also be mandatory in the sense that it is required for other purposes, such as membership in professional associations and societies, staff development and in-service training activities undertaken as a

Table 1. Growth in Mandatory Continuing Education Related to Licensure,
1980–1984

Professional Group	Number of States in 1980	Number of States in 1984	Percent Growth
Architects	1	1	
Certified public accountants	36	43	19
Dentists	9	10	11
Engineers (professional)	1	2	100
Lawyers	9	12	33
Nurses	11	11	
Nursing home administrators	43	44	2
Optometrists	44	46	5
Psychologists	8	12	50
Pharmacists	21	33	57
Physical therapists	3	3	
Physicians	20	18	(–10)
Real estate sales-persons and brokers	14	22	57
Social workers	10	18	80
Licensed practical/vocational nurses	11	10	(–9)
Veterinarians	22	24	9

NOTE: The information displayed in Table 1 is based primarily on data provided by Louis
E. Phillips, University of Georgia. States include the District of Columbia.

part of internal institutional quality control procedures, promotion and salary increase decisions, or special professional recognition at the national level (such as the Physician's Recognition Award of the American Medical Association) or at the state level (such as the Connecticut Pharmaceutical Association Continuing Education Recognition Award).

Generic Mandation. In short, an entire educational system has emerged that is built on the expectation that professionals will be systematically involved in continuing education. This development has resulted in a generic state of mandatory continuing education as a professional norm, and it has spawned significant academic and practitioner interest in the educational community (Green and others, 1984; Houle, 1980). Regardless of one's position on the traditional understanding of mandatory continuing professional education as a prerequisite for periodic relicensure, mandatory continuing professional education has become a fact of contemporary professional life that is having an undeniable impact on educational practice and generating new and increasing responsibilities for continuing educators (Knox, 1984; Mattran, 1981).

Education as Big Business. As the expectation of participation in continuing education has spread, the marketplace for educational programs for professionals has grown. A broad marketplace for continuing education for credit has developed outside our traditional credit- and recognition-granting institutions, such as colleges and schools and their extension divisions, which have long been leaders within the community of continuing education providers. Continuing professional education is now being offered by a wide spectrum of organizations for which education has not been historically a primary activity but for which it is becoming an area of increasing interest, activity, and commitment. As a result, it is not surprising that this young and burgeoning service industry would be subject not only to significant internal competition and struggle (Stern, 1983) but to rules and regulations designed to assure that educational programs meet quality standards. It is in this manner that educational programs can be shaped to serve the interests of the professions: by assuring high-quality programs that meet specific educational expectations and standards within a framework for accountability and public recognition.

Competition. As in any enterprise, one must be competitive in continuing professional education in order to be successful. Because accreditation recognizes the professional value of an educational program, it plays an important role in the program's marketability. An understanding of the accreditation context has become in many instances a crucial element of competitive and successful educational practice. The remainder of this chapter familiarizes the reader with accreditation and some of its overall implications for the practice of continuing professional education.

The Emergence of Standards of Practice

The emergence of quality standards for continuing professional education is a relatively recent phenomenon. The first formal development of standards occurred in medicine in the early 1960s. These standards have evolved into the current *Essentials and Guidelines for Accreditation of Sponsors of Continuing Medical Education* administered by the Accreditation Council for Continuing Medical Education (1982). Quality standards for continuing professional education proliferated throughout the 1970s. A recent study (Council on the Continuing Education Unit, 1983) reviewed continuing education standards for a wide variety of professionals, including certified public accountants, chiropractors, dentists, engineers, lawyers, librarians, physicians, nurses, nursing home administrators, pharmacists, psychologists, public health administrators, real estate appraisers, respiratory therapists, and social workers. For this chapter, examples are drawn primarily from dentistry, medicine, nursing, and pharmacy, although the observations made and the implications discussed are generally applicable to most of the groups just cited.

Intended Beneficiaries of Standards

The standards for quality that have been developed for continuing professional education in the professions are intended to serve a variety of constituencies. First, they are intended to serve their respective professions in that they provide a self-regulating and quality control mechanism. Second, the standards are designed to serve professional practitioners by providing a framework for assurance of reasonably high-quality educational programs. In this sense, being accredited is a public mark of quality that a professional community accepts as an important endorsement of program acceptability.

Third, the standards provide a resource to regulatory bodies in the same way that traditional accreditation of professional degree programs does; as a quality assurance mechanism, standards provide the basis for identifying programs that can be viewed as having acceptable quality for the purposes of meeting various educational requirements for licensure. That quality makes such programs more marketable.

Fourth, standards provide a framework for the responsible practice of continuing professional education. In this way, they can act as a primer or training guide for individuals who have responsibility for developing continuing professional education programs but who have little or no formal training or experience in continuing education. Finally, standards serve the best interests of the public by promoting quality programs for professionals who hold the public trust.

Major Responsibilities

Continuing professional educators operating under accreditation standards must perform two major roles effectively. The first of these is that of manager of information within a framework of accreditation-related documentation and educational accountability. Programs must be administered and information must be handled in a manner that will enable the educator to demonstrate responsible educational programming in full compliance with the letter of the applicable set of quality standards (McInnes and Green, 1984). The second role is that of manager of education; in this role, the educator addresses the spirit of existing quality standards. To the continuing education practitioner, these two areas of responsibility may not always seem to be compatible. However, the challenge of assuring their compatibility is one of the most important responsibilities of the continuing professional educator.

Management of Information. Developing continuing professional education activities within an accreditation framework is an information-intensive, record-keeping endeavor. Continuing education accreditation mechanisms and the audits and reviews to which they subject continuing professional educators and their institutions are of two basic types. Accreditation can be built on a provider approval mechanism that closely follows the traditional model of accreditation. In this approach, an accrediting agency evaluates the capabilities of a providing organization (such as a school, hospital, or association) to develop programs in accord with the established standards for educational quality. This approach, which is sometimes referred to as sponsor approval, places the primary emphasis on the institution or organization that produces and provides programs. Providers or sponsors that receive approval are expected to develop programs in accord with educational quality standards, and they are periodically evaluated, audited, or both in order to assess their level of compliance and to recommend modifications necessary to assure future compliance.

The second approach is built on a program approval model that is predominately regulatory in scope. As the name implies, this approach involves the evaluation of particular continuing education programs, usually on a prospective basis. The review produces a judgment regarding quality—usually before the program is first offered. Programs that are found to meet the established standards are designated as approved and allowed to be offered for credit; programs that are not approved are not acceptable for credit.

As Table 2 shows, provider approval is far more widely accepted and used than program approval, in large part due to the fact that it reflects both regulatory and educational interests. It is easier to evaluate an institution than it is to evaluate each of the continuing education programs that the institution plans to offer. Provider approval also enables an accreditation agency to provide guidance and help continuing education providers to improve their educational programs. In contrast to the program approval approach, which often limits the approval process to shortsighted consideration of products (the educational programs themselves) after they have been developed, provider approval looks not only at the programs but at all aspects of the educational mechanisms that contribute to quality program development and implementation. Thus, provider approval can include evaluation of administrative and organizational structures, budget, staff, program and instructional materials, development procedures, faculty selection criteria, faculty guidance activities, faculty reward structures, cosponsorship frameworks, facilities used for program production and program implementation, program evaluation activities, and data utilization protocols. Compliance with quality standards in the provider approval process often involves a variety of organizational and procedural improvements that will help to maintain and improve the quality of future programs.

Management of Education. In the light of all the structural and informational demands that accreditation systems place on providers, how does a program developer get any educational work done? In addressing this key question, it is important to note that one reason for the emergence of quality standards is the often limited educational background and expertise of individuals who occupy positions of educational responsibility within providing organizations. As a result, individuals with solid continuing education training are in an especially good position to offer guidance and leadership in reconciling the informational and educational management roles inherent in the practice of continuing professional education.

Reconciliation of Roles. Both creativity and flexibility are important in reconciling the two roles. While continuing professional educators may

Table 2. Approaches to Accreditation

Accrediting Organization	Provider Approval	Program Approval
American Association for Respiratory Therapy	X	X
American Council on Pharmaceutical Education	X	
American Dental Association[a]	X	
American Institute of Real Estate Appraisers	X	
American Medical Association	X	
American Nurses' Association	X	X
American Psychological Association	X	
American Public Health Association		X
Association of Continuing Legal Education	X	
Council for Noncollegiate Continuing Education Administration	X	
Council on Chiropractic Education		X
Engineers Council for Professional Development	X	
National Association of Social Workers	X	
National Council on Quality Continuing Education for Information, Library, and Media Personnel	X	

Source: CCEU Reporter, 1983, 5 (1), 1-4.
[a]Approval mechanism no longer in effect.

seem to face markedly different sets of standards, the standards may prove to be relatively similar. The major differences are far more likely to be administrative than educational in nature. Differences among sets of standards encountered can usually be addressed without major modifications in the core planning process or program development protocols. As a result, any differences that exist can be effectively addressed largely through the management of information and the packaging of educational programs.

Economy and coordination in working with multiple sets of standards require program design and development processes that already reflect the components that the various sets of standards share. These common denominators of the planning process can enable continuing educators to build some degree of economy into their program planning and development protocols. Within the context of accreditation, systematic attention to these components constitutes a practical approach that a well-trained continuing educator should be able to administer in an efficient and effective manner. The remainder of this section addresses five areas of expectation. For each area, I describe the prevailing or emerging point of view represented by existing quality standards and briefly describe the implications of these expectations for continuing professional educators.

Promotional Materials. Most standards speak to the development of promotional materials. Based on the principle that promotional material should enable professionals to engage in informed program selection, promotional literature is often expected to provide a substantial amount of information. To illustrate this point, Table 3 documents the requirements for promotional literature that have been established in dentistry, medicine, nursing, and pharmacy. Emphasis on promotional literature is a pervasive element of quality standards. A recent study of twenty-three sets of standards (Council on the Continuing Education Unit, 1983) found that only four did not make reference to promotional literature; of the remaining nineteen sets, all but two included detailed references.

One problem created by standardized expectations in this area is that sufficient planning time is needed to ensure that all required aspects of program-related promotion and information dissemination are solidified well in advance of program implementation. Another problem flows from the likelihood that increased attention to detail in promotional literature may result in a refined and more exact description of the intended targeted audience. While this focusing may result in more educationally sound programs, it may also narrow profit margins, increase tuition and fees, and render one's educational programs less price-competitive. A related difficulty, discussed by Scanlan in Chapter Seven, is the ethical dimension of program promotion.

One approach to dealing with the tension between responsible and ethical program promotion on the one hand and marketability on the other is to attend carefully to educational need assessment and target audience segmentation with a view toward stratified marketing strategies (Kotler, 1975). A related approach is the coupling of general topics that would be of interest to multiple professions with specific tailoring, or "educational packaging," that meets the needs of particular groups of professionals that sensitive need assessment and stratified marketing have identified.

The "educational packaging" just mentioned involves revisions that allow a program for one audience to be transformed into a program for a different audience. For example, a basic course in client communications could be packaged to form the basis for a patient education program for physicians. By modifying the learning objectives, reworking the educational materials, establishing new examples, or developing alternative learning assessment activities, developers could later repackage the program so that it could become the core for a patient counseling program for pharmacists. The concept of educational packaging is an important educational management strategy for competitive and effective practice within the context of accreditation.

Table 3. Promotional Literature Information Requirements

Required Information	Profession			
	Dentistry	Medicine	Nursing	Pharmacy
Content description	X	X	X	X
Learning objectives	X	X	X	X
Target audience	X	X	X	X
Schedule of activities	X			X
Cost to the participant	X		X	X
Refund policy				X
Credit to be awarded	X			X
Faculty members	X	X	X	X
Faculty qualifications	X			X
Identification number(s)				X
Sponsor name statement (standardized language referring to recognition by the accrediting agency)	X	X	X	X
Educational prerequisites of participants	X	X		
Instructional methods to be used	X	X		

Learning Objectives. The second common denominator among quality standards is the expectation that learning objectives will be developed for each program. The pervasiveness of this expectation is illustrated by the Council on the Continuing Education Unit (1983) study, which found that only one of the twenty-three sets of standards reviewed did not reference goals and objectives; of the remaining twenty-two sets, all but one provided direct and in some cases detailed references to learning objectives.

It is generally expected that learning objectives will be written in a fashion that provides criteria for evaluation of program success. The development of such objectives is generally seen as appropriate in the early stages of program planning. This expectation is consistent with such classic views of educational planning as those of Tyler (1949), Knowles (1970), and Houle (1972), who see educational objectives as curricular or programmatic templates.

An alternative conception of educational objectives is that they are educational promises made to prospective participants by planners on which the program will deliver. This fundamentally ethical point of view is consistent with the overall expectation that continuing professional education will foster outcomes that are relevant to improvement in professional practice. In this sense, program planning becomes a matter of making and fulfilling educational promises.

Again, making and fulfilling such promises is in many instances a matter of educational packaging: Educational objectives are used to organize an educational activity and present it in an orderly, systematic, and understandable fashion. Contrary to traditional and often parochial views, under which the development of learning objectives is a component of the early planning process, objectives as educational promises can be developed before, during, or even after the learning activity has been designed. In fact, there may be instances in which it would be both prudent and educationally sound not to make educational promises until late in the planning process. This could be the case when the planner had limited input from faculty and little influence in the development of instructional design and materials. While it might be argued that the planner was not really acting as an educator in such a case but rather as a coordinator or facilitator, it could still be an educationally sound decision to delay the establishment of educational objectives. If the reader prefers, the process can be thought of as one of "refining objectives [that] have been inherent since [the learning activity] was first contemplated and have usually been somewhat clarified during the process of decision" (Houle, 1972, p. 136).

The concept of making educational promises emphasizes the educator's ethical responsibility to fulfill learners' expectations. It also highlights the need to avoid the trivialization of educational objectives that occurs when planners haphazardly generate shallow and largely factual-recall-type objectives (for example: "As a result of participation in this program, you will be able to list five new antibiotics"). At the same time, small successes are important, and modest objectives, preferably focused on application of professional knowledge and skills to practice, are both appropriate as educational promises and legitimate as educational objectives.

Content Relevance. What is perhaps the dominant concern in the program development area is nonprocedural in character. This is the concern for the relevance of content. It has two aspects: First, the content must be relevant to the particular professionals for whom the program is being planned. This requirement suggests that each profession has a contemporary working understanding of its subject matter that programs must address. The resulting curricular territory is often defined in continuing education quality standards. However, the definitions contained in standards often address ranges of topics, which provides only a general mapping of acceptable topic areas and lacks specificity. For example, the American Council on Pharmaceutical Education (1985) defines topics relevant to the contemporary practice of pharmacy to include the socio-economic, behavioral, legal, and administrative aspects of health care delivery; the causes, treatment, and prevention of diseases; the properties, actions, dosage forms, and therapeutic applications of drugs; and the pharmacologic assessment, monitoring, and management of patients. As a result, it is useful for program developers to consult with one or more members of the targeted profession for advice on questionable, marginal, or emerging topics.

A second, related aspect involves assuring that a topic is presented in a manner that is relevant to practice. As continuing professional educators address this aspect of content relevance, the prospects of multidisciplinary programs or of programs that could be repackaged for multiple professional audiences often become attractive. However, it is generally recommended that close intitial contact be sought with the appropriate accrediting agencies in such cases in order to assure that content is developed in keeping with the prevailing understanding of the curricular territory.

Program Evaluation. The fourth area common to quality standards is the expectation of program evaluation. It is generally expected that providers will evaluate the success and quality of the educational programs they offer and that the resulting data will be analyzed and systematically used to improve existing programming or to justify future programming.

A general weakness in this area is that program evaluation rarely goes much beyond the level of a happiness index. While an indication of overall satisfaction can be a legitimate and valuable indicator for program planning (Kenny, 1981), the educational superficiality of such data may not lend adequate support to the improvement of educational programs in a substantive sense.

This is an area where continuing professional educators can provide leadership. As Knox points out in Chapter Five, the use of effective program evaluative approaches and the systematic use of results have potential for significant contributions. In this area, special attention to what Bloom (1980) has called "alterable variables"—program elements that can be manipulated in future programs in an effort to achieve desired improvements in program quality—is recommended (Kenny and Harnisch, 1982).

Learning Assessment. The fifth area common to quality standards is the expectation that a meaningful form of learning assessment will be offered in conjunction with each program. Commonly, some measure of achievement of the program's learning objectives is required.

This expectation can be addressed from two points of view. First, learning assessment is often seen as an objective measure of achievement from which the provider can gain some valid, reliable, and objective indication of the effectiveness of the program in achieving its promised educational objectives. Second, learning assessment can also be seen as a participant-based learning activity that gives program participants an opportunity to assess their learning systematically, "try out" what they are learning, and receive some form of structured feedback on their performance.

At the present time, posttests are often used to satisfy this expectation. However, participants are often reluctant to be tested. Such resistance is understandable. The challenge for continuing professional educators is to blend the two points of view to yield learning assessment exercises that provide valid and objective data that can be used both to assess program effectiveness and to offer rich and nonthreatening learning experiences. Success in meeting this challenge is likely to involve both an enhancement of participants' involvement in the learning process and an increased focus on subject matter applications to practice.

In view of efforts now being made in several professions to identify and refine practice competency statements and to develop forms of competency assessment testing, success in meeting this challenge is crucial. Such testing may threaten to bring continuing professional education down to the level of teaching to the test and reduce the richness currently found in the competitive marketplace for continuing professional education.

A related challenge for continuing educators, which Knox discusses in Chapter Five, involves the development of ways of documenting self-directed learning in a manner that will provide acceptable evidence for professional recognition and credit whether applications are related to licensure or not. This is an especially significant challenge, because continuing educators could provide strong leadership and guidance to the accreditation community by developing educationally sound approaches to documentation that are learning experiences in their own right: these approaches to documentation would have to incorporate the principles of education for adults.

Conclusion

The degree to which evolving standards of practice in continuing professional education enhance its prospects for future development depends in part on the ability of continuing educators to accommodate a diversity of expectations. Because continuing educators practicing in the service of the professions compete both with traditionally trained educators and educational specialists, such as educational psychologists and instructional development specialists, and with noneducators, they need to address the educational expectations that quality standards have established. They also need to deliver on educational promises and to provide leadership and guidance in support of the accreditation community. Meeting these challenges requires a new flexibility and a commitment to the development of educational programs that address the needs and expectations of professionals, their professions, consumers of professional services, and the formalized blending of these needs and expectations embodied in the accreditation standards of today and tomorrow.

References

Accreditation Council for Continuing Medical Education. *Essentials and Guidelines for Accreditation of Sponsors of Continuing Medical Education.* Chicago: Accreditation Council for Continuing Medical Education, 1982.

59

American Council on Pharmaceutical Education. *Criteria for Quality*. Chicago: American Council on Pharmaceutical Education, 1985.

Bloom, B. S. "The New Direction in Educational Research: Alterable Variables." *Phi Delta Kappan*, 1980, *61*, 381-385.

Council on the Continuing Education Unit. "Progress Report on Standards Project." *CCEU Reporter*, 1983, *5* (1), 1-4.

Green, J. S., Grosswald, S. J., Suter, E., and Walthall, D. B., III (Eds.). *Continuing Education for the Health Professions: Developing, Managing, and Evaluating Programs for Maximum Impact on Patient Care*. San Francisco: Jossey-Bass, 1984.

Houle, C. O. *The Design of Education*. San Francisco: Jossey-Bass, 1972.

Houle, C. O. *Continuing Learning in the Professions*. San Francisco: Jossey-Bass, 1980.

Kenny, W. R. "The Role of Context-Specific Information in the Management of Continuing Professional Education: An Exploratory Study." Unpublished doctoral dissertation, University of Illinois at Urbana-Champaign, 1981.

Kenny, W. R., and Harnisch, D. L. "A Developmental Approach to Research and Practice in Adult and Continuing Education." *Adult Education*, 1982, *33*, 29-54.

Knowles, M. S. *The Modern Practice of Adult Education: Andragogy Versus Pedagogy*. New York: Association Press, 1970.

Knox, A. B. "Epilogue: Further Strategies for Strengthening Continuing Education for the Health Professions." In J. S. Green, S. J. Grosswald, E. Suter, and D. B. Walthall, III (Eds.), *Continuing Education for the Health Professions: Developing, Managing, and Evaluating Programs for Maximum Impact on Patient Care*. San Francisco: Jossey-Bass, 1984.

Kotler, P. *Marketing for Nonprofit Organizations*. Englewood Cliffs, N.J.: Prentice-Hall, 1975.

McInnes, J. M., and Green, J. S. "Information Systems that Meet Management Needs." In J. S. Green, S. J. Grosswald, E. Suter, and D. B. Walthall, III (Eds.), *Continuing Education for the Health Professions: Developing, Managing, and Evaluating Programs for Maximum Impact on Patient Care*. San Francisco: Jossey-Bass, 1984.

Mattran, K. J. "Mandatory Education Increases Professional Competence." In B. W. Kreitlow and Associates, *Examining Controversies in Adult Education*. San Francisco: Jossey-Bass, 1981.

Stern, M. R. (Ed.). *Power and Conflict in Continuing Professional Education*. Belmont, Calif.: Wadsworth, 1983.

Tyler, R. W. *Basic Principles of Curriculum and Instruction*. Chicago: University of Chicago Press, 1949.

W. Robert Kenny is associate executive director of the American Council on Pharmaceutical Education (ACPE) in Chicago, Illinois; director of the ACPE Continuing Education Provider Approval Program; and adjunct assistant professor in the College of Pharmacy, University of Wisconsin.

A realistic approach to program evaluation can enhance the quality of continuing educators' decision making.

Evaluating Continuing Professional Education

Alan B. Knox

Planners and providers of continuing professional education are regularly faced with the need to make decisions regarding their programming and to choose among alternative ways of solving problems or attaining desired goals. Ultimately, such decisions depend on judgments of worth or merit of the process or program in question. To the extent that such judgments are based on systematic efforts to define criteria, collect relevant information, and analyze its meaning, continuing professional educators are engaging in the informed decision-making process of evaluation.

Although few will argue against the need for improved evaluation, it remains one of the most widely neglected and little-used processes in today's educational systems (Worthen and Sanders, 1973). Among the most important reasons for this neglect is ambiguity about the appropriate role, purposes, methods, and procedures of educational evaluation. Such ambiguity is particularly evident in the evaluation of continuing professionall education. Given the diversity of goals, methods, and assumptions underlying the delivery of continuing professional education outlined by Scanlan in Chapter One and the growing demands for quality assurance mechanisms reviewed by Kenny in Chapter Four, it is little wonder that providers are seeking clarity in regard both to the need for and to the appropriate use

R. M. Cervero, C. L. Scanlan (Eds.). *Problems and Prospects in Continuing Professional Education.* New Directions for Continuing Education, no. 27. San Francisco: Jossey-Bass, September 1985.

of educational evaluation. This chapter places evaluation in perspective and provides practical guidance to practitioners of continuing professional education who wish to improve the quality of their decision making.

The Focus and Purpose of Evaluation

Like those engaged in any systematic effort to attain a particular end, continuing professional educators should begin their evaluation activity by carefully delineating its focus and purpose. In regard to clarifying the focus of evaluative efforts, Grotelueschen (1980) suggests that practitioners should address three preliminary questions: Who are the audiences for evaluation findings? To what program-related issues should the evaluation effort respond? What scope, focus, and timing is likely to help guide decision makers' actions? Answers to these three questions help to narrow the scope of the evaluation effort and assist the planner in identifying its primary purpose.

Among the many purposes that educational evaluation can serve, those of justification, improvement, and planning are most relevant to the continuing professional educator. Follow-up studies assessing the impact of past programs can enhance accountability and serve to justify the continuation of program support to policy makers, program sponsors, and contributors (Knox, 1979). Ongoing program evaluation can enable people associated with the program to assess the effectiveness of current efforts for purposes of program improvement (Knox, 1969). Needs assessment shows how evaluation can help to plan future efforts (Pennington, 1980). Although some evaluation studies may include all three purposes, most studies are kept manageable and useful by limiting the focus to a single purpose.

Another basis for specifying evaluation purposes is the decisions that users expect to base on the findings. For example, individual professionals can use feedback, critiques, and self-assessments to conduct self-directed learning projects and enhance their performance. Learners, instructors, and coordinators associated with a specific continuing professional education program can use program evaluation findings to strengthen program decision making in such issues as selection of topics, methods, or materials. Program administrators can use evaluation findings to assure quality and increase benefits for those who are served.

Various resources are available to help continuing professional education practitioners make decisions about the focus and purpose of evaluation. In addition to general books, articles, and monographs on educational evaluation, there are writings on evaluation approaches specifically applicable to continuing education (Grotelueschen, 1980). Guidelines and criteria designed for the evaluation of continuing education programming include the *Principles of Good Practice in Continuing Education* disseminated by the Council on the Continuing Education Unit (1984) and the quality elements for continuing education of health professionals originally developed by Suter and others (1981).

Beyond providing detailed guidelines for the development and evaluation of continuing professional education programs, these resources emphasize the importance of specifying the focus and purpose of evaluation. Achieving clarity on these dimensions increases the likelihood that those associated with programming will participate in the evaluation process and ultimately use its findings to improve their decision making.

Methods and Procedures

Having reached consensus regarding the focus and purpose of the evaluation effort, the continuing professional educator should choose an appropriate methodological framework. Many methods and procedures apply to the conduct of an evaluation, whether the setting is individual (such as supervisory coaching or correspondence study), temporary group (such as a course or workshop for people from various locations), or organizational (Anderson and Ball, 1978; Belasco and Trice, 1969; LeBreton, 1976; Stake, 1967; Worthen and Sanders, 1973). The next section provides guidelines for evaluation in any setting. The following sections review special considerations in the evaluation of self-directed learning, evaluation for program improvement, and evaluation to assess the impact or effect of continuing professional education.

Basic Guidelines

After developing a clear understanding of the audiences for the evaluation (such as participants, instructors, administrators, policy makers) and the questions that need to be addressed, the educator can develop an evaluation plan that encompasses the project's scope, its approach, and the procedures necessary for data collection and analysis.

Scope. An evaluation study can be conducted on almost any scale. An informal study can take but a few hours and dollars. Such an evaluation can be based on trend information assembled from existing records and on conversations with a few people who occupy places that allow them to know about program functioning and impact. The findings can be reported in a one-page memo or in a conversation with an administrator. A formal evaluation on the same topic could expend more resources than those used by the program itself. Such an evaluation could entail external evaluation specialists, development of new forms for data collection, and use of elaborate data analysis procedures to guarantee valid and detailed findings.

On what basis can decisions be made about the scope and scale of evaluation? Two questions are germane here: How risky are the decisions that evaluation findings will be used in making, and how much is already known? A major feasibility study can be justified for a professional association that is investing significant resources in the development of a prototype workshop and materials to be used by local chapters. In contrast, only a modest evaluation effort seems warranted when earlier evaluations and much anecdotal experience with the clientele, content, and methods are used to fine-tune an ongoing continuing professional education program.

Another way of deciding on the scope and scale of an evaluation project is to select the program elements or planning aspects that need emphasis. Grotelueschen (1980) suggests that any evaluation can address four elements of the program—participants, instructors, topics, and context and four aspects of the planning process—goals, plan, implementation, and outcomes. When these two dimensions are combined to form a matrix, each of the resulting sixteen cells suggests questions that an evaluation study can answer. For one program, evaluation might focus on the accommodation of participants' and instructors' goals in a mutually satisfactory plan. For another program, evaluation might focus on contextual influences (such as practices of associations and employers) that affect the efforts of participants to apply what they learn in the program in the work setting. Review of such a matrix can suggest which cells warrant highest priority.

Another way of focusing an evaluation effort is to select standards of achievable best practice in the planning and conduct of continuing professional education. This procedure is similar to the procedure used in needs assessment whereby standards of professional practice are compared with current performance to identify discrepancies on which the educational program should focus. Selected characteristics of professionalization (Houle, 1980) or quality provider elements (Green and others, 1984) could serve as standards and criteria for the evaluation of program development and administration. This approach is similar to the practice employed by external accrediting agencies, which Kenny describes in Chapter Four. Having such standards and criteria helps to identify existing and new indexes of current program functioning and thus provides a basis for data collection.

Approach. An evaluation plan also needs to reflect the general approach to be taken that can guide data collection and analysis (Worthen and Sanders, 1973). Three features of the evaluation approach need to be considered: whether the evaluation is oriented toward past, present, or future; what emphasis needs to be given to the interests of each audience of the evaluation; and how involved in the process each audience should be.

Past-oriented summative evaluation studies contribute to justification and accountability. Such studies include the follow-up study, self-study followed by external review for accreditation, and evaluation research studies by outside specialists (Cook and Reichardt, 1979). This approach emphasizes impact and benefits and the impartiality of external evaluators.

Present-oriented formative evaluation studies contribute to program change and improvement (Eisner, 1976; Guba and Lincoln, 1982; Knox, 1969). Studies of this nature include self-studies, self-assessments, action research, feedback to participants or instructors aimed at encouraging and reinforcing progress, and refinement of materials or procedures. This approach emphasizes informal efforts by people closely associated with the program to study procedures they use in ways that encourage use of findings for improvement.

Future-oriented needs assessments contribute to planning (Pennington, 1980). Such assessments include secondary analysis of work-related records, surveys, advisory committee input, market research, evaluation of pilot projects, and preferences of past participants for future programs. This approach emphasizes multiple sources of information, including potential participants and others. Evaluation for planning seeks to specify the preferences and expectations of potential participants and other people who are supporters or beneficiaries of the program so that mutually beneficial exchange can occur.

In all three approaches, the audience for evaluation findings can be people closely associated with the program, such as participants, instructors, or program administrators; people more distant from day-to-day program operation, such as administrators in the parent organization, policy makers, funders, or the general public; or some combination of the two. When the audience is mainly insiders, it may be relatively easy to encourage them to use the findings; however, they will have to be shown that the findings are impartial. When the audience is mainly outsiders, it is relatively easy to be impartial; however, efforts will have to be made to connect findings with constructive change strategies. In either instance, if the main audience is not inclined to use evaluation findings, the evaluation approach should help its members to develop the understanding and sense of ownership needed to assure their active involvement. Procedures for increasing involvement include establishing advisory committees, soliciting opinions by interview, and providing an opportunity to respond to evaluation plans and preliminary findings.

Data. As already noted, evaluation consists of making judgments based on data or evidence about the worth or effectiveness of continuing professional education programs in ways that encourage people associated with them to use the findings for planning, improvement, or justification. The quality of the judgments that are made and the likelihood that they will be used are contingent on the effectiveness with which relevant evidence is collected and analyzed.

An evaluation study of a specific continuing professional education program will use only a few of the many data collection procedures that are available. There are two main differences between data collection for continuing professional education and for other types of educational programs for adults, such as adult basic education: the relative ease with which educational interventions can be related to specific aspects of job performance, and the capacity of professionals themselves to relate to often complex data collection procedures. Many evaluation data are descriptive and provide the basis for comparisons and analysis that lead to judgments of worth or effectiveness. Collection of useful data depends on the awareness of desirable alternatives from which to select as well as on considerations of feasibility and accessibility.

Evaluation data include such things as statements of goals, records of participation, opinions about materials, and evidence of impact, such as improved practices. The quality of data is affected by their pertinence to the issues and audiences for the report as well as by technical considerations, such as validity and reliability. Other considerations include efficiency, unobtrusiveness, and redundancy for key variables. Data sources include program personnel (participants, instructors, administrators), other people familar with program functioning, and records (of attendance, finances, and work performance and findings from other reports and studies). Procedures for data collection include interviews, questionnaires, testing, summary of existing records, and observation. Criteria for selection of data collection procedures include type and source of data, study purposes and audiences, timing, and resources. Standard references on the collection of research and evaluation data apply to evaluation of continuing professional education (Becker and Geer, 1960; Cook and Reichardt, 1979; Gordon, 1975; Worthen and Sanders, 1973).

The selection of data analysis procedures depends on purpose, audiences, expertise, and resources. Attention to data analysis in the evaluation plan is important so that data are collected in a form appropriate for the intended analysis. If an informal evaluation is to help a program administrator discover whether a satisfactory continuing professional education program can be improved, data analysis may consist of a portrayal of program functioning that combines a descriptive overview with opinions on suggested improvements solicited from those associated with the program. For an external assessment to help policy makers decide whether to increase support for a long-term program or phase it out, data analysis may consist of time series trend lines comparing enrollments, finances, and participant satisfaction ratings with data for similar programs and projections based on new developments in the field. For a follow-up study to draw convincing conclusions about the impact of a program on performance, data analysis may compare former participants with a control group of comparable nonparticipants regarding changes in performance that can reasonably be attributed to participation in the continuing professional education program and respondents' perceptions of the extent to which such educational experiences changed their performance.

This section has addressed general procedures for the design of evaluation studies and for the collection and analysis of data. In specific instances, the focus, scope, approach, and design depend on purpose, audience, and resources. The next three sections illustrate evaluations specifically for self-directed learning, program improvement, and impact evaluation.

Self-Directed Learning

Many writers deeply concerned about continuing professional education have emphasized the importance of self-directed learning and assessment (Brown and Uhl, 1970; Green and others, 1984; Houle, 1980; Knox, 1974; Miller, 1967). Professionals can be helped in a number of ways to assess their educational needs and to select the individual strategies most likely to assist them in updating, maintaining, or improving their levels of performance. The appropriate strategies include self-assessment inventories, performance audits, and simulations, such as in-basket exercises and patient management problems.

Because of their emphasis on the solution of practical problems, self-directed learning strategies require evaluative approaches wholly different from those commonly employed in other settings. As applied among health professionals (Barrows and Tamblyn, 1980), this problem-based approach integrates learning and evaluation so that learners can interpret and use information continually to assess their proficiency. In such a context, the evaluator's role is to assist the professional in documenting progress by establishing relevant standards, providing useful feedback, and encouraging persistence and application of learning.

One of the most promising methods of assessing individual problem-solving proficiencies is the simulation exercise. Although such exercises vary widely in format and construction, they closely approximate the actual processes that professionals use in formulating a problem, gathering information, generating hypotheses, and selecting from alternative solutions.

Other aspects of performance that may require individualized evaluative efforts include professionals' consideration of time, cost, and follow-up strategies; technical and communicative skills; interpersonal relations; and the conceptual and knowledge bases underlying practice. Many of these elements of performance are amenable to existing methods of evaluation (for example, performance audits for follow-up strategies, self-assessment inventories for knowledge adequacy). For others (for example, interpersonal relations), wholly satisfactory methods have yet to be developed.

In addition to assessing the process and the results of professional performance, evaluation can be used to assess the effectiveness of professionals' self-directed learning efforts. Such evaluation uses findings to improve the efficiency or effectiveness of such efforts. Evaluation of self-directed learning can focus on a professional's ability to define the learning problem, to select its focus, to use appropriate resources (personnel, material, time), and to achieve desired goals.

Ultimately, those who evaluate self-directed learning activities must recognize that there are many ways of achieving a given goal. Nonetheless, it is necessary for educators and professionals alike to be able to identify and apply criteria useful in judging both the process and the outcomes of individual learning. Such criteria should address components of the problem-solving process, attend to the specialized field of professional practice in which the problem is encountered, and account for the unique context in which professionals apply their skills.

Program Improvement

Most practitioners who help to plan and conduct continuing professional education programs do so on behalf of a provider, such as a professional association, university, or employer. Such providers commonly use program evaluation to improve their program offerings (Knox and Associates, 1980). If such formative evaluation occurs, it is typically planned and conducted by program administrators with cooperation from instructors, other resource persons, planning committee members, and sometimes evaluation specialists. This section reviews the use of evaluation for purposes of improving continuing professional education programs. It includes some examples, guidelines, and suggested resources.

Most of the basic guidelines presented earlier apply fairly well to formative evaluation for improvement of continuing professional education offerings. The greatest impediments in practice are either the absence of appropriate evaluation materials (they are expensive to create) or a lack of familiarity with existing materials. For continuing professional education in the work setting, records regarding work performance (patients' records in a hospital, production rates in a factory, sales figures in wholesale or retail trade) can be used as outcome measures with which the effectiveness of particular educational interventions can be assessed.

When an entire range of program offerings is evaluated, it is necessary to do more than sum the evaluation of individual programming efforts. This is because the success of a provider's overall effort depends on the provider's ability to develop, market, fund, and build support for its programming. Unfortunately, as the operation increases in complexity, it becomes less amenable to comprehensive evaluation. One way of handling the complexity is to decentralize the evaluation effort and review some of the offerings each year with attention to the larger administrative and organizational context as well as to individual offerings. Self-studies and external reviews are well suited to comprehensive program evaluation and usually occur in conjunction with a larger accreditation effort, as Kenny notes in Chapter Four. Externally funded programs sometimes receive more detailed evaluation, in part because it is required, in part because it is supported as a budget item.

Many resources are available to strengthen formative evaluation. Such major providers as universities, professional associations, and employers commonly use professionals experienced in the planning and conduct of sophisticated evaluation studies. However, overemphasis on technical details and precision in evaluation processes can discourage the educator from getting started. Small in-house evaluative efforts are better than none at all; practitioners can and should develop the basic skills necessary to conduct their own formative evaluations. The most useful resources on program evaluation include Belasco and Trice (1969), Grotelueschen (1980), Guba and Lincoln (1982), LeBreton (1976), Stake (1967), and Worthen and Sanders (1973).

Impact Studies

Another purpose of evaluation is to assess the extent and type of impact that a continuing professional education program has on subsequent performance by participants, on the clientele that they serve, or on the organizations with which they are associated. Impact evaluation includes follow-up studies of former participants and review of time series performance data aimed at detecting improvements that can be attributed to educational participation. There are sufficient instances of impact evaluation in continuing professional education that general guidelines can be suggested and examples can be noted (Green and others, 1984; Knox, 1979; Stein, 1981).

The first step is to decide whether the educational intervention is powerful enough to produce a major change in occupational performance. When the intervention seems insufficient, it is usually a waste to conduct an impact evaluation study. By contrast, when the intended outcomes are realistic and reasonably attainable, impact assessment is feasible. The collection of information related to impact is facilitated by the existence of accepted standards of achievable best practice and by work-related records that reflect the quality of performance.

The major difficulty in assessing the impact of continuing professional education lies in documenting improvements in performance (and in related benefits to others) that can at least in part be attributed to participation in educative activity. This effort leads to a dilemma. Naturalistic approaches (which evaluate actual programs with a minimum of intervention) are most feasible, and their findings are most likely to apply to similar programs that are not greatly affected by the evaluation process (Guba and Lincoln, 1982). However, the absence of experimental controls makes it difficult to attribute impact to the program (Cook and Reichardt, 1979). Impact evaluation studies can produce valid and useful findings if these guidelines are followed:

First, specify accepted standards of achievable best practice as criteria against which discrepancies from current practice (needs) and improvements in practice (application) can be assessed.

Second, select or develop valid and feasible indexes of optimal performance, which are sufficiently associated with complex and elusive outcomes of continuing professional education that they can serve as criteria in assessments of program impact. (The identification, specification, and validation of such indexes is an area of high priority in continuing professional education evaluation.)

Third, use a time series approach to collect performance index data. The time series approach allows differences in performance before, during, and after participation to be documented.

Fourth, establish at least one comparison sample of nonparticipant practitioners with which the group of participants can be compared.

Fifth, obtain from participants their subjective perceptions of program influence on the criterion measures of performance. Compare these findings with the more objective data previously collected. Cross-validated findings are usually more persuasive than either kind of finding alone.

Sixth, use various types and extents of educational programming for comparable samples (or for samples during successive stages) to assess the extent and type of impact on performance and related benefits. In a cost-benefit impact study of continuing education for emergency room physicians, the impact on practice (benefit) increased greatly as the treatment changed from provision of information, to discussion of implications for improved practice, to inclusion of administrators in the interest of organizational support for desirable changes (Knox, 1979).

Conclusion

All continuing professional education programming undergoes evaluation, at least in the informal sense. However, when a high level of confidence in the validity of judgments is desirable, more rigorous approaches to evaluation are necessary.

Most effective evaluation studies focus on selected program aspects and seek to answer important and timely questions. The findings are usually used to plan, improve, or justify a specific program. Although comprehensive, in-depth evaluation studies are rather difficult to conduct, their findings can serve broad purposes, such as indicating the extent of impact that well-designed programs can have. Comprehensive evaluation studies can also provide guidelines for the design of future programs that are likely to have an impact.

The contrast between ringing declarations about the importance of evaluation for planning, improving, and justifying continuing professional education and the small portion of programs for which any useful evaluation occurs can be cause for discouragement. Part of the problem may be the rhetoric. The ideal that evaluation specialists advocate tends to be so elaborate and rigorous that it seems to be unfeasible. Perhaps the more viable approach is to use continuous but selective program evaluation to monitor program functioning and results (Green and others, 1984). When a lean monitoring activity identifies a program aspect that warrants substantial improvement, intensive evaluation can be used to aid in the process.

This chapter has emphasized that evaluation can help practitioners of continuing professional education to strengthen their program development practices regarding planning, improvement, and justification. However, useful evaluation can benefit other groups interested in quality programming. Individual professionals can benefit from the resulting improvements in existing programs. Evaluation can also help them to assess the likely benefits of participation and to guide their own self-directed learning activities. Other audiences for evaluation findings include policy makers and the general public. Both groups are seeking greater accountability in the delivery of continuing professional education. Of course, each evaluation study can address only a limited number of audiences and issues. Collectively, however, program evaluation can address the entire range of audiences and issues so that higher-quality programs are provided, and the professions, their individual members, their employers, and society as a whole are well served.

References

Anderson, S. B., and Ball, S. *The Profession and Practice of Program Evaluation.* San Francisco: Jossey-Bass, 1978.
Barrows, H. S., and Tamblyn, R. M. *Problem-Based Learning.* New York: Springer, 1980.

Becker, H. S., and Geer, B. "Participant Observation: The Analysis of Qualitative Field Data." In R. N. Adams and J. J. Preiss (Eds.), *Human Organization Research*. Homewood, Ill.: Dorsey Press, 1960.

Belasco, J. A., and Trice, H. M. *The Assessment of Change in Training and Therapy*. New York: McGraw-Hill, 1969.

Brown, C. R., Jr., and Uhl, H. S. M. "Mandatory Continuing Education: Sense or Nonsense?" *Journal of the American Medical Association*, 1970, *213*, 1660-1668.

Cook, T. D., and Reichardt, C. S. (Eds.). *Quantitative and Qualitative Methods in Evaluation Research*. Beverly Hills, Calif.: Sage, 1979.

Council on the Continuing Education Unit. *Principles of Good Practice in Continuing Education*. Silver Springs, Md.: Council on the Continuing Education Unit, 1984.

Eisner, E. W. "Educational Connoisseurship and Criticism: Their Form and Functions in Educational Evaluation." *Journal of Aesthetic Education*, 1976, *10*, 135-150.

Gordon, R. L. *Interviewing: Strategy, Techniques, and Tactics*. (Rev. ed.) Homewood, Ill.: Dorsey Press, 1975.

Green, J. S., Grosswald, S. J., Suter, E., and Walthall, D. B., III (Eds.). *Continuing Education for the Health Professions: Developing, Managing, and Evaluating Programs for Maximum Impact on Patient Care*. San Francisco: Jossey-Bass, 1984.

Grotelueschen, A. "Program Evaluation." In A. B. Knox and Associates, *Developing, Administering, and Evaluating Adult Education*. San Francisco: Jossey-Bass, 1980.

Guba, E. G., and Lincoln, Y. S. *Effective Evaluation: Improving the Usefulness of Evaluation Results Through Responsive and Naturalistic Approaches*. San Francisco: Jossey-Bass, 1982.

Houle, C. O. *Continuing Learning in the Professions*. San Francisco: Jossey-Bass, 1980.

Knox, A. B. "Continuing Program Evaluation." In N. Shaw (Ed.), *Administration of Continuing Education*. Washington, D.C.: National Association for Public School Adult Education, 1969.

Knox, A. B. "Lifelong Self-Directed Education." In R. J. Blakely (Ed.), *Fostering the Growing Need to Learn*. Rockville, Md.: Division of Regional Medical Programs, Bureau of Health Resources Development, 1974.

Knox, A. B. (Ed.). *Assessing the Impact of Continuing Education*. New Directions for Continuing Education, No. 3. San Francisco: Jossey-Bass, 1979.

Knox, A. B., and Associates. *Developing, Administering, and Evaluating Adult Education*. San Francisco: Jossey-Bass, 1980.

LeBreton, P. (Ed.). *The Assessment and Development of Professionals: Theory and Practice*. Seattle: University of Washington, 1976.

Miller, G. E. "Continuing Education for What?" *Journal of Medical Education*, 1967, *42*, 320-326.

Pennington, F. C. *Assessing Educational Needs of Adults*. New Directions for Continuing Education, No. 7. San Francisco: Jossey-Bass, 1980.

Stake, R. E. "The Countenance of Educational Evaluation." *Teachers College Record*, 1967, *68*, 523-540.

Stein, L. S. "The Effectiveness of Continuing Medical Education: Eight Research Reports." *Journal of Medical Education*, 1981, *56*, 103-110.

Suter, E., Green, J. S., Lawrence, K., and Walthall, D. B. "Continuing Education of Health Professionals: Proposal for a Definition of Quality." *Journal of Medical Education*, 1981, *56*, 687-707.

Worthen, B. R., and Sanders, J. R., *Educational Evaluation: Theory and Practice*. Belmont, Calif.: Wadsworth, 1973.

Alan B. Knox is professor of continuing education, University of Wisconsin-Madison. A frequent writer on the education of adults in general and on the evaluation of professional education in particular, he is current president of the American Association for Adult and Continuing Education; he also chairs the Commission on Leadership of the National University Continuing Education Association.

Interorganizational collaboration in continuing professional education is a fact of life. A knowledge of the process can prove useful in building more effective linkages.

Interorganizational Collaboration in Continuing Professional Education

Lillian Hohmann

Continuing professional education is achieving a new level of maturity. This maturity represents a refinement of ongoing processes in the field. One of its major forms, interorganizational collaboration, is the subject of this chapter. Until now, collaboration has been mostly a practical art, and relatively little systematic thought has been given to the best ways of achieving its intent. However, as continuing professional education continues to grow and develop, collaborative arrangements will become increasingly more common and essential to its effective delivery.

Meaning and Extent of Collaboration

As Cervero, Bussigel, and Hellyer note in Chapter Two, educators are beginning to respond to the increasing complexity of professionalism. They recognize the need for developing both the individual and the profession. This recognition has made it necessary to evaluate the particular strengths of different providers. A wide variety of organizational responses has been the result. Collaboration is one of many important organizational responses. Collaboration is the decision of two or more organizations that

R. M. Cervero, C. L. Scanlan (Eds.). *Problems and Prospects in Continuing Professional Education.* New Directions for Continuing Education, no. 27. San Francisco: Jossey-Bass, September 1985.

serve one or more professions to combine their resources to meet specific educational goals over a period of time. Not all joint organizational ventures are collaborative, nor is collaboration the answer to all problems in continuing professional education, but it is an important tool that can extend the resources of institutions.

Collaboration is a complex issue that is beginning to be understood apart from particular fields and special educational problems. Collaboration has been explored as a side issue—in continuing medical education, for example—or it has been described as a delivery mechanism for a particular educational method (Houle, 1980). Until recently, knowledge of collaboration has been descriptive and generally overshadowed by other educational concerns.

Cervero (1984) uses Beder's (1978) theoretical framework of interorganizational relationships or linkages to describe the continuing professional education unit in a large Midwestern university. Beder argues that the success of an adult education agency depends on its ability to secure resources, such as participants, money, information, power, and domain, from its environment. According to Beder, resources are secured through strategically planned interorganizational linkages. The case study shows the circularity involved in securing participants to guarantee income that is used to develop a broad program that helps to establish domain, power, and prestige, which all serve to attract more participants to the programs. Beder's framework is useful for looking at the macroenvironment, for it articulates the general factors critical in mounting a large multiprogram agency, and it suggests the complexity involved in establishing such linkages.

The need for achieving a better understanding of the process of collaboration was the motive for a survey of 247 organizations belonging to the National University Extension Association and the Educational Section of the American Society of Association Executives (Hohmann, 1980). The study found that 90.5 percent of the universities and 94.3 percent of the associations surveyed engaged in continuing professional education; 92.6 percent of the universities and 49.6 percent of the associations reported collaborative relationships. The survey explored organizational aspects and perceived benefits and problems of collaboration. The central problem area for both types of organizations was not any specific educational issue (curriculum, faculty, evaluation) but the issue of defining turf.

The survey summary comments are as pertinent today as they were five years ago: "The respondents shaped their responses in a way that the planners had not anticipated. They pointed to the individual behavior of administrators—the sorting out of hierarchies and turfs and finding professional friendship. . . . This mixed bag of clues may require further separation into special issues for consideration. For example, what kinds of persons are drawn to the administration of continuing education . . . ?

How do their environmental settings either foster or inhibit the development of professional strategies to enter cooperative relationships? What skills are necessary to the development of exceptional continuing education programs and to the development of mutually rewarding multiorganizational enterprises? . . . The survey respondents spoke so clearly to the point of personal dynamics in cooperative relationships that, however fragmented future research efforts are on this problem, this one area should not be overlooked" (Hohmann, 1980, p. 22).

Collaboration is not a completely rational process of matching up organizations that have complementary needs and resources. Besides representing a significant organizational venture and a peculiarly personal experience, it is a quintessential political process. For even the most modest joint undertaking in continuing professional education, the shape and form of its delivery and much of its outcome have been shaped by the adjustment of subgroups within each participating organization. These subgroups become competitive forces in a complex environment composed of considerable opportunities and threats.

Trends and Implications for Collaboration

Changing Perception of Competence. The increased concern about competence and education for optimum performance of practitioners has strengthened assessment and educational techniques. However, these techniques have been expensive to develop and to deliver, which suggests that there may be many more years of "traditional" programming before such methods can be fully embraced. Nevertheless, the significance of the trend does not rest solely on the prospect of delivering a different type of educational experience to practitioners; it also may stimulate new and different kinds of relationships among providers and ultimately lead to greater coherence in the field.

Professional Interdependence. The second major trend is the growing recognition of interdependence among the professions. While the very process of professionalization is one of individuation and separation of roles, notions of teamwork in the health professions, engineering, education, social work, and other fields have all but mandated crossover educational experiences—the type of continuing professional education in which members of different professions come together as learners. As professions mature, their members become freer to move past the struggle for identity toward integration with other professionals as peers. Such integration provides an opportunity to view competence from an interdisciplinary perspective.

Chenault and Burnford (1978) discuss the idea of integrated human services education, which they say the future will demand. Chenault's organic model of preservice education, in-service education, and continuing education includes horizontal aspects (across professions, organizations, systems, and communities); vertical aspects (from paraprofessionals to professionals, from recipients to providers, from individual citizens to local communities and federal programs); and interrelational aspects (interrelationships among the elements just named, interrelationships that are more complex than mere accumulations of uni- and bidirectional relationships). However idealistic the viewpoint expressed by Chenault may be, it is clear that continuing educators have an important role in play in facilitating such integration and that collaboration among providers of continuing professional education may be one of the most viable ways of achieving this intent.

Professional Maturity. The third major trend is the changing perception of professional maturity that recognizes the impact of personal and professional stress and career growth on practitioners. Professionalism is more than the sum of techniques and skills learned in school and perfected in practice. It depends on successful maturation of the individual through identifiable and predictable phases. Such programs as career planning, stress management, substance abuse education, and personal goal planning have generally not been considered part of continuing professional education. Indeed, it may be several years before they achieve any significant stature. However, as researchers delve deeper into the meaning of competence and the barriers to excellent performance, programs such as these may be pivotal to attempts to improve our definitions of professional maturity.

Continuing Professional Education Marketplace. Private practice is becoming a romantic memory as increasing numbers of lawyers, physicians, architects, accountants, and engineers practice in organizations and on teams composed of specialists. The impact on the providers of continuing professional education is important, for, as choices about goals and beneficiaries must be made, it becomes clear that it is more efficient to target organizations rather than individuals.

A Case Study of Collaboration

An important source of insight into collaboration issues has been a study at the Pennsylvania State University (Lindsay and others, 1981); the study, known as the Continuing Professional Education Development Project, was funded by the W. K. Kellogg Foundation. This five-year research and development effort seeks to foster practice-oriented continuing professional education with the long-term expectation of developing collaborative relationships between academic and professional organizations. It is based on the Practice Audit Model developed at Penn State in collaboration with the pharmacy profession (Smutz and others, 1981). The current project involves six professions: accounting, clinical dietetics, architecture, nursing, clinical psychology, and medicine. The collaborators include university faculty from each profession, representatives of state and national associations in those fields, and project staff. In combination, these collaborating individuals represent a profession team.

The six teams began their work in 1981 and spent two years developing and field testing the profession practice description. Each team planned a practice audit session for a sample of practitioners. Each audit session used a variety of assessment tools. Analysis of results has led to judgments regarding performance deficiencies that could be remedied by continuing professional education. In 1984, the teams planned and delivered their first cosponsored continuing education programs.

Role of Boundary Spanners in Collaboration. While the project is not yet complete, there has already been one helpful outcome: the work by Smutz (1984) on "boundary spanners"—individuals designated by organizations to represent them in interorganizational relationships. Smutz's subjects were the university and association representatives involved in the Penn State project.

Smutz's conceptual framework is political; thus, he is interested in boundary spanners' communication within their organizations, not in their personal traits. Smutz suggests that boundary spanners are important instruments of organizational change not only because they bring ideas from outside their organization but because they evaluate and interpret new ideas and introduce them selectively to individuals or groups. The control of information and access to leadership are pivotal in shaping organizational decision making.

Measures of boundary spanners' performance included the amount of communication, the mode of communication (oral or written), the form of communication (formal or informal), message recipients, and content of communication. In general, boundary spanners provide brief (less than one page for written or less than ten minutes for oral) messages to both organizational members (opinion leaders) and organizational contacts (superiors). Messages tend to be oral rather than written.

Smutz found that boundary spanners' communication changes in kind and amount over time. Early in the change process, information provided to the organization tends to be descriptive and infrequent. Evaluative commentary becomes more prevalent as new ideas begin to take shape. However, not all boundary spanners regard their roles in the same way. While most agree on delivering descriptive or evaluative information, only half engage in prescriptive communication with their organization. It is interesting that the communication of boundary spanners within the organization is predominantly verbal.

High-performing boundary spanners had an extensive background in the profession (though not necessarily in continuing education) and communicated frequently within their organizations. High-level position and amount of influence were important characteristics of boundary spanners in nonacademic organizations, but these characteristics were not important for boundary spanners as a group. Smutz found that boundary spanners who represented academic institutions communicated less within their organizations than boundary spanners in other professional organizations. He explained this finding by the value constructs and operational characteristics of academia—faculty autonomy, low internal communication, and orientation to discipline rather than organization.

Smutz concluded that boundary spanners can affect the outcome of an interrelationship in significant ways through their interpretation of ideas and their influence over opinion leaders. Thus, it would be desirable to exert as much influence as possible over the choice of an organizational representative, even to the point of developing selection criteria. Smutz suggests that considerable printed information can be provided to augment the skills of those whose experience in the field is limited or those whose performance as boundary spanners (as indicated by low frequency of communication) seems doubtful.

Another important finding was that organizations tend to select representatives on the basis of their perceived need either to expand or protect their continuing education domain. Organizations that attempt to protect their domain send persons with high continuing education expertise in low-level positions who communicate minimally and who have relatively little influence within the organization. Organizations that attempt to expand their domain send high-level professional experts who communicate frequently within the organization and who have influence. Interestingly, these individuals tend not to have expertise in continuing education. Smutz suggests that organizations that plan to expand their programs are the most likely candidates for collaboration and that an important clue to their intentions is the level of staff sent to a planning meeting.

Key Issues in Collaboration. Although boundary spanners are highly important in collaborative arrangements, there are other issues that demand attention. In their study of collaboration, the Penn State staff found the literature on interorganizational relations to be useful in developing a model of concept and decision. The model suggests that there are five key issues in the building of relationships between organizations: the form of interaction, the climate and preconditions, the determinants, the agreement, and the linkage mechansim (Lindsay and others, 1981). A summary of each issue followed by one application illustrates techniques useful in establishing effective collaboration.

Form of Interaction. The form of interaction can range from complete organizational independence to a merger of organizations. Three types of interaction are commonly described: cooperation (ad hoc assistance), coordination (working together while retaining considerable autonomy), and collaboration (working together jointly and continuously toward a specific goal).

The form chosen determines the depth of commitment as measured by time and resources expended and by scope of goals; however, the commitment need not be equal between organizations. One of the challenges of collaboration is to find a balance between autonomy and involvement and to sustain the organizing force or goal. At Penn State, the important force is the Practice Audit Model.

The Practice Audit Model is the pivotal tool for focusing discussion between those representing the university and those representing practitioners. The utility of this tool can be discussed at two levels: the macroenvironment and the microenvironment of collaboration in continuing professional education.

One of the difficulties of planning continuing education across professions is the tendency of each profession to regard itself as unique and to turn inward when developing its programs. This tendency limits collaboration and diminishes the contributions that others could make. Use of the practice audit with seven professions confirms what continuing educators have long asserted: that each profession need not go it alone in planning continuing education.

In the microenvironment sense, the model provides a mechanism that accurately identifies deficiencies within each profession. Based on the belief that practitioners do not always recognize their deficiencies, the practice audit uses several assessment tools, including case studies, pen-and-paper exercises, and videotaped simulations. Practitioners participate in the assessment sessions, and they are evaluated by profession teams. From those assessments come the priorities for joint program development.

The Practice Audit Model is not without limitations. It is too expensive and lengthy for some professional groups, and it is perhaps too complex for many university-based continuing education units to mount. Furthermore, it does not pretend to meet the individual goals of learners except through the sensitivity of the leaders selected to conduct the programs. What it does extremely well is to help continuing professional educators engage in a directed discussion about competencies of practitioners that is less subject to the pitfalls of traditional needs analysis. Traditional methods that have common sense and intelligent observation at their core need not be eschewed, but new tools can be used to refine them. The directed process that uses representatives from academia and the field creates greater potential for conflict as scrutiny of the profession intensifies, but the process of conflict and its resolution may be an important prerequisite of efforts to confront the problems of joint program delivery.

Climate and Preconditions. As open systems, organizations depend in varying degrees on their environments to gain resources and deliver products. In general, an organization is more inclined to change behavior—and to interact with other organizations—in proportion to its environmental changes.

The need for universities to reach into the adult student community in the face of diminishing enrollment requires little further evidence or discussion. For the Penn State project, Pennsylvania professions and their associations were researched to uncover the most likely candidates for joint planning in continuing education. According to one study, it is more typical for professional associations to seek cooperative relationships with universities than it is for universities to seek such relationships with associations. On a question asking how collaborative relationships started, 36.6 percent of the association respondents reported that they sought out universities, while 28.2 percent reported that both groups intentionally sought each other out. Of the university respondents, 29.4 percent reported that association staff sought out university staff, and 38.1 percent reported that both groups intentionally sought each other out. A smaller proportion of respondents (14.4 percent of the association representatives and 22.2 percent of the universities) reported that university staff had sought out the association staff. Who seeks out whom in collaboration provides important clues to an organization's domain-expanding or domain-protecting activity.

Determinants. Organizations can be motivated to collaborate by resource shortages or because an opportunity to expand their programs is presented. However, moving from a general interest to a particular collaboration requires more impetus from determinants—factors making specific organizations form specific commitments. Some of the most important determinants are domain consensus (each organization retaining its "territorial" rights), perception of gain (a perception held by each organization), and possession of sufficient reserve resources (resources that are not critical to the organization's survival).

The Penn State project translated determinants into selection criteria. Guidelines and criteria established by project staff were used to develop a formal selection process, and a systematic analysis of potential cooperating organizations was conducted to find appropriate candidates. The thirty selection criteria helped to assess the capacity of a university or association to commit itself to the goals of the project. These criteria accounted for such factors as expertise, strength of interest, delivery systems, critical mass of practitioners, resources available, and previous or current work in role delineation.

A demonstration project might be more highly structured than other ventures, yet it suggests the importance of objective criteria in differentiating between potential collaborators and those whose needs and resources are incompatible. Detailed criteria also help to prevent midstream disappointments based solely on poorly defined expectations of the other agency and entry into collaborations based solely on the personal compatibility of agency leaders. Organizations that are considering collaboration need to develop criteria for such arrangements well in advance of searching for partners.

Agreements. Agreements are formal commitments specifying such elements as amount and type of resources and the balance of exchange between organizations. Agreements can range from informal memoranda to highly formal legal contracts drawn up to protect the domain of each participant. The formality of an agreement in the legal sense is less an issue than the depth of understanding between the staffs of organizations regarding their responsibilities. The responsibilities and resource commitments for the Penn State project are extensive and were thoroughly documented at the outset. The specific duties of project staff, academic faculty, and association staff were expressed in terms of expertise, time commitment, and product/activity involvement (writing, planning, administration). Three levels of responsibility were specified: major, shared, and supplementary. Regardless of the extent of the particular collaboration, a written agreement on specific organizational responsibilities and program and fiscal arrangements (both input and outcomes) is important.

The process of developing an agreement is important in that it can confirm the initial perceptions of resource exchange or reveal misperceptions. It follows that organizations having the clearest understanding of exchange units have the greatest chance of success.

Linkage Mechanisms. Linkage mechanisms are the highly or loosely structured links between organizations—the who, when, and how of concrete communication—that are selected by the groups involved. Generally, the less formalized the linkage, the more collegial the relationship, and the greater the need to provide methods of reducing conflict.

How two organizations develop linkages determines both the outcome of the relationship and the quality of its process. Linkages are the who and what of collaboration, the face-to-face transactions. They can be formal and limited, or they can be loosely defined. A loosely defined linkage promotes democracy and creativity within the group, but it also creates potential for conflict and ultimately for failure.

At Penn State, one key linkage mechanism was a group process leader who assisted each team during the early stages of organizing its work. The project leaders recognized that ownership of the process, group cohesion, and commitment depend on early transfer of power and authority from the organizers to the total group. The neutrality of the group process professionals was instrumental in making such transfer occur.

Adult educators who are skilled in group process may not see any need to exclude themselves from that function during planning meetings. However, clarity of communication is so vital to collaboration that one person may be usefully designated to serve only that goal.

Conclusion

Some changes result from random and nonspecific interaction in the environment. However, significant change—the kind of organizational

84

response required to meet a new understanding of competence, interdependence of professions, professional maturity, and organizational marketing—cannot depend only on random interaction.

The preceding description of one major collaborative effort is optimistic because it illustrates the balance involved in thinking about the education issues of our day, about organizational change, and about the persons who will be leaders of change. Larson (1977, p. 244) clearly identifies the challenges that lie ahead: "The autonomy and the 'intelligence of the whole' traditionally vested in professional work appear to be, now, uncertain privileges. To build or defend monopolies or competence and access does not protect these intrinsic qualities. For this, professional workers, in solidarity with all workers, must find the means of claiming and realizing the full human potential of all work."

Collaboration is arduous business, but its merit transcends the delivery of programs. Its benefit lies in its power to broaden the often narrow conceptions that particular professional groups bring to bear on what, ultimately, are common issues and concerns. Our best hope for change lies in continuing dialogue.

References

Beder, H. W. "An Environmental Interaction Model for Agency Development in Adult Education." *Adult Education*, 1978, *28*, 176–190.

Cervero, R. M. "Collaboration in University Continuing Professional Education." In H. Beder, (Ed.), *Realizing the Potential of Interorganizational Collaboration.* New Directions for Continuing Education, no. 23. San Francisco: Jossey-Bass, 1984.

Chenault, J., and Burnford, F. *Human Services Professional Education: Future Directions.* New York: McGraw-Hill, 1978.

Hohmann, L. *A Survey of Cooperation Between University Extension Divisions and Professional Associations to Provide Continuing Education for the Professions.* Unpublished report in Continuing Education for the Professions project, National University Extension Associates and the University of Chicago, 1980.

Houle, C. O. *Continuing Learning in the Professions.* San Francisco: Jossey-Bass, 1980.

Larson, M. S. *The Rise of Professionalism: A Sociological Analysis.* Berkeley: University of California Press, 1977.

Lindsay, C. A., Queeney, D. S., and Smutz, W. D. *A Model and Process for University/Professional Association Collaboration.* University Park: Continuing Professional Education Development Project, Pennsylvania State University, 1981.

Smutz, W. D. "Formal Boundary Spanners and Organizational Change: Establishing University/Professional Association Interorganizational Relationships." Unpublished doctoral dissertation, Pennsylvania State University, 1984.

Smutz, W. D., Lindsay, C. A., and Queeney, D. S. *The Practice Audit Model: A Process for Continuing Professional Education Needs Assessment and Program Development.* University Park: Continuing Professional Education Development Project, Pennsylvania State University, 1981.

A former Kellogg Fellow at the University of Chicago, Lillian Hohmann serves as a continuing education consultant to business organizations and educational institutions. She has held administrative and reseach positions in both the voluntary association and the university sectors.

Only by clearly delineating basic principles of human values can continuing professional education practitioners effectively respond to the moral dilemmas they encounter.

Ethical Issues in Continuing Professional Education

Craig L. Scanlan

Continuing professional educators assume a diversity of roles and often serve many different constituencies. Conventional knowledge and experience and extant standards of good practice are generally adequate to ensure that they fulfill these roles competently and that the needs and expectations of the constituencies whom they serve are indeed met. However, special circumstances can arise in which prevailing rules and standards provide an insufficient basis for our choices and actions (Frankena, 1973). More often than not, these special circumstances involve conflicting assumptions over the rights and obligations that ought to govern human relationships. Conflicting value premises are clearly evident in the following situations:

- A provider of continuing professional education must decide between organizing a program around perceived growth needs expressed by a group of professionals and their conflicting "real" needs as identified by measures of performance deficits
- An advisory committee recommends that a client education program replace the professional development efforts currently being employed to address inequities in an organization's service delivery
- A staff trainer charged with updating the technical skills of the organization's professional employees is given the choice between

R. M. Cervero, C. L. Scanlan (Eds.). *Problems and Prospects in Continuing Professional Education.* New Directions for Continuing Education, no. 27. San Francisco: Jossey-Bass, September 1985.

a voluntary andragogical approach to intervention and a mandated behavioral strategy using negative sanctions to ensure compliance

- A professional licensure board requests that a continuing professional education agency submit participation and performance records for a practitioner charged with incompetence.

In each of these situations, the continuing professional educator is faced with a dilemma posed by conflicting obligations or competing rights. Resolution of such dilemmas demands qualitative insight and judgments wholly different from those governing the more technical aspects of continuing professional education practice. Understanding and confronting what are fundamentally moral issues requires skill in ethical reasoning.

The Need for Ethical Reasoning in Continuing Professional Education

In light of the increasing emphasis being placed by the educational community on the analysis of professional ethics, it is ironic that academia in general and continuing professional education in particular have paid so little attention to the moral issues underlying their practices (Dill, 1982; Singarella and Sork, 1983). The American Association of University Professors required more than half a century to evolve a code of ethical behavior for academicians; the resulting code has often been criticized for its archaic treatment of the moral issues inherent in the professorial role (Scriven, 1982). Only recently has the continuing education community even acknowledged that it needs ethical principles to guide its practice (Mason, 1979). Unfortunately and all too often, such perspectives represent overly simplistic or proscriptive notions of how to deal with patent misbehavior or flagrant abuses of authority (for example, plagiarism, student exploitation, sexual harassment) over which few would disagree (Callahan, 1982).

The really difficult moral decisions stem from situations in which two or more right choices are incompatible, in which the choices represent different priorities, or in which limited resources exist to achieve the desired priorities (Callahan, 1982). Due in part to the growing complexity of our education systems, the proliferation of clientele groups being served, and the continually changing expectations of clientele, educators are facing both an increasing number and an increasing diversity of such moral dilemmas. Moreover, certain unique attributes of continuing professional education—for example, its typically marginal status within parent organizations, its reliance on multiple linkages with external agencies, and its business and marketing orientations—compound the influence of these general educational factors and increase the potential for values conflicts

(Stern, 1982). Only by applying sound principles of ethical reasoning can the continuing professional educator resolve these conflicts in consistent and morally justifiable ways.

The Nature of Ethical Reasoning

Any consideration of ethical principles eventually must address the meaning of such terms as *right, good,* and *obligatory.* Obviously, in the absence of some benchmark of what constitutes morally justifiable behavior, it is possible to argue in favor of almost any position (Chambers, 1981).

Normative ethics is the branch of moral discourse that addresses the "rightness" of our judgments and actions and that provides guidance in confronting moral dilemmas. The difficulty is that normative ethics is not a well-indexed code of prespecified behaviors; rather, it represents several different systems of reasoning, which can provide conflicting perspectives on the moral justifiability of our choices. The differences in reasoning are most evident when we compare the two dominant approaches to normative ethics: consequentialism and formalism. This chapter will use the following case example to explicate these two modes of ethical reasoning:

> A provider of continuing professional education, intent on maximizing the desirability of a particular program, has applied for but not received formal confirmation of the professional accreditation necessary to offer approved credit for this activity. No prior program submitted to the agency by the provider has ever been denied approval. Rather than hold up printing (which is already behind schedule), the provider considers including notice of program accreditation in the promotional brochures.

Consequentialist Perspective. From the consequentialist perspective, the basic criteria by which we judge rightness or wrongness in a situation such as the one just portrayed is the relative amount of good (over evil) that a particular action brings into being (Frankena, 1973). The good to which morally right conduct is a means is most often conceived in terms of nonderivative values, such as human happiness or self-actualization. The most common application of consequentialism, which is also called utilitarianism, judges acts according to the principle of utility; the aim is to promote the greatest general good for all involved.

As applied to the our case example, utilitarian reasoning would require the provider to sum the relative value and disvalue brought into being for each alternative action for all those affected (the client group, those whom its members serve, the continuing professional education agency, the professional association, and so forth). That one of the alternatives under consideration involves the untruthful promotion of the program's status would be a consideration in calculating its utility only if the consequences of such an action meaningfully figured into the equation. Given the high likelihood that the program will be approved, this act of untruthfulness is probably both temporary and inconsequential in nature. Moreover, notice of program approval is likely to increase participation of the targeted client group, which will directly benefit the providing agency. Assuming that the program itself is of high quality and that it meets the expectations of those who are involved, increased participation is likely to result in more widespread benefits to the client group and, by implication, to those whom its members serve. Conversely, omitting notice of program accreditation or stating truthfully that the application was in process might have a negative impact on participation and thus not provide comparable benefits to the provider, client group, and those whom its members serve. The provider who applied utilitarian reasoning would probably conclude that promoting the program as approved would result in the greatest good for the greatest number and that it was thus the most morally justifiable (and obligatory) of the available alternatives.

Critics of consequentialist reasoning claim that the approach suffers from two fundamental flaws: First, the "calculus" involved in projecting and weighing the amount of good over evil resulting from alternative actions is at best complex and at worst impossible. Second, reliance on the principle of utility to the exclusion of all else can result in actions that are incompatible with ordinary judgments regarding the rights and obligations inherent in human interactions.

Formalist Perspective. Formalist or deontological thought denies what consequentialist reasoning affirms. That is, formalist thought asserts that certain features of an act itself, other than just the value that it brings into being, determine its moral justifiability (Frankena, 1973). Within this framework, standards of right and wrong are formulated in terms of basic principles or rules that function apart from the consequences of a particular action. An act is judged morally justifiable if and only if it upholds the rules or principles that apply.

Contemporary ethical principles underlying modern formalism have evolved from many sources, including the conceptions of natural law espoused by Aristotle and Aquinas, Judeo-Christian formulations of morality, Kant's analysis of universal duties, and the values orientations characterizing modern political systems, especially those embodied in our democratic form of governance. Although some controversy exists, most ethicists can agree that autonomy, beneficence, and justice are guiding principles in formalist approaches to moral decision making.

The principle of autonomy obliges us to uphold others' freedom of will and freedom of action. The principle of beneficence obliges us to further the interests of others either by promoting their good or by actively preventing their harm. The principle of justice obliges us to ensure that others receive what they rightfully deserve or legitimately claim. Embodied in each duty is a correlative right, that is, the right to autonomous choice, the right not to be harmed, and the right to fair and equitable treatment. From these general principles of rights and obligations one can generate specific rules applicable to specific situations, for example, confidentiality, consent to personal interventions, truth telling, and so forth.

The emphasis that formalism places on the intrinsic characteristics of actions clearly addresses the primary shortcoming of utilitarianism, namely its frequent incompatibility with ordinary judgment. The major objection to formalist reasoning lies in its potential for inconsistency. Critics of formalist reasoning object, first, that no principle or rule can be framed that does not admit of exceptions, and second, that no set of principles or rules can be framed that does not admit of conflicts (Frankena, 1973). Indeed, no formalist has ever presented us with a conflict- or exception-free set of principles.

Acknowledging these concerns, Ross (1930) suggested that conflicts among principles could be resolved by differentiating between actual and prima facie duties. An actual duty represents what we actually ought to do in a given situation; actual duties admit of exceptions. In contrast, a prima facie duty holds without exception and is always a right-making characteristic of our judgments and actions. All things being equal, prima facie duties are equally binding. In the event of conflict, one must determine the weight or priority of competing principles to ascertain what is one's actual duty.

Applying this refinement of formalist reasoning to the dilemma described in this chapter, we can see that our prima facie duty to further the interests of the provider agency, its clients, and those whom its members serve (the principle of beneficence) is in conflict with our prima facie duty to be truthful in our interactions with others (the principle of veracity, derived from concepts of justice and autonomy). Our actual duty depends on the relative priority that we give to these principles. If our obligation to be truthful in our interactions with others outweighs our duty to further their best interests (as many would claim that it does), then we are morally obliged to portray the program's approval status honestly, even though fewer benefits may accrue to those involved. From this perspective, the act of untruthful promotion should be considered morally wrong even if the program subsequently gained approval.

Mixed Approaches. Mixed approaches to moral reasoning attempt to capitalize on the strengths inherent in these two major lines of ethical thought. Rule utilitarianism, a variation of consequentialist thought, represents one such approach. Like most consequentialist theories, rule utilitarianism emphasizes the centrality and value of rights and obligations in moral reasoning (Frankena, 1973). To the rule utilitarian, the question is not which act or practice has the greatest utility but which rule or principle would promote the greatest good if it were generally accepted. As in formalist thought, conflict among two or more applicable principles is addressed by assigning priority to them. In contrast to formalist reasoning, in which hierarchy is usually determined by intuitive logic, rule utilitarianism establishes priority among principles according to their relative utility.

In considering the morally justifiable course of action in our dilemma of program promotion, the rule utilitarian, like the formalist, would weight the competing principles of veracity and beneficence. Unlike the formalist, however, the rule utilitarian would ascribe a value to these principles that derived from their usefulness as a means to a given end. Upholding the principle of veracity is useful to the extent that it promotes trust and good faith in human interactions, a necessary prerequisite to helping interventions such as continuing professional education. Similarly, upholding the principle of beneficence ensures that those whom we serve can be confident that, at a minimum, our actions will not result in their harm. Under the assumption that furthering others' best interests is contingent on the establishment and maintenance of a trusting relationship, the rule utilitarian would probably conclude that upholding the principle of veracity would promote the greater good, even if in this particular situation truthful promotion would not lead to the best possible consequences.

Among alternative modes of moral reasoning available to the continuing educator, the rule utilitarian approach is probably the most appealing and useful. Its appeal derives in part from its ability to address both the human rights and obligations and the consequences inherent in our actions. Moreover, rule utilitarianism seems best able to accommodate the modern realities of human experience that so often impinge on the day-to-day practice of continuing education.

Ethical Reasoning and Reality. Proponents of ethical theories are often (and rightly) criticized for their abstract treatment of morality. If ethical reasoning is to be of any value to those who must apply its concepts, it must account for the reality of human experience and take its rightful place among the many considerations that compete for our attention. These considerations include facutal premises and beliefs (for example, that one mode of instruction is more effective than another), legal concepts (for example, contract theory), and externally imposed mandates or expectations (for example, continuing professional education accreditation standards). In many instances, such considerations uphold our underlying moral convictions and serve to strengthen support for a given decision or action. The real challenge to the practitioner of continuing professional education arises when moral principles dictate one course of action and factual knowledge, legal concepts, or external expectations dictate another. In addressing the applications of moral reasoning in the following section, the reader should consider the underlying realities of each situation and the extent to which such considerations uphold or refute the moral point of view.

Applications to Practice

The application of ethical reasoning to continuing professional education practice is best addressed by differentiating between sources of values conflict common to continuing professional education and education in general and sources of values conflict unique to continuing professional education. Major sources of values conflict common to continuing professional education and education in general evolve from the conception of education as a means of social intervention. Major sources of values conflict unique to continuing professional education evolve from its special organizational characteristics. This section raises ethical issues stemming from these sources and suggests some approaches that can be used to resolve them.

Continuing Professional Education as a Social Intervention. Kelman and Warwick (1978) define a social intervention as any act that attempts to alter the characteristics of individuals or the pattern of relationships between them. Under this conceptualization, both education in general and continuing professional education in particular represent methods of social intervention. Four major ethical issues stem from the application of social intervention strategies: the choice of goals to which the change effort is directed, the definition of the target of change, the choice of means used to implement the intervention, and the evaluation of the consequences of the intervention (Kelman and Warwick, 1978).

The four dilemmas presented in the first section of this chapter provide examples of each issue. They will be used here to explicate various applications of ethical reasoning.

Choosing Goals. The most fundamental of all value judgments in education is the choice of goals to which efforts are directed. Chapter One of this volume elaborates on the various goal orientations characterizing continuing professional education, but draws no conclusions regarding their appropriateness. Ultimately, however, continuing professional educators must focus their efforts on the achieving of some desired ends, *desired* in the sense that they are consistent with personal or agency values.

The first situation described in this chapter requires the educator to choose between two quite different goals, fostering growth or remediating deficiencies. Assuming that the desired focus is on individual professionals (as opposed to an organization or a system), a utilitarian would carefully delineate the potential consequences of each alternative, giving consideration to the relative amount of good brought into being for professionals on the one hand and for the agency on the other. Factors that might be involved in the decision could include the personal satisfaction of professionals, the number of professionals who are likely to participate, the continued ability of the agency to serve them, and the relative impact of the alternatives on the professionals' careers. Summing the relative goods on each factor for each alternative would probably result in a decision to attend to the professionals' felt needs, not the "real" needs.

In contrast, for the formalist or rule utilitarian, the forced choice between goal orientations presents a conflict between valued principles. Attending to the perceived needs of the professionals would uphold their rightful claim to freedom of will and action (the principle of autonomy), yet it might at the same time fail to further their best interests (the principle of beneficence). Alternatively, addressing their real needs for updating or improved performance attends to their best interests, but it may compromise their right to choose freely. In order to resolve the dilemma, both the formalist and the rule utilitarian would defer to a preestablished hierarchy of principles. It seems likely that both would choose to prioritize autonomy over beneficence, although they would have distinctly different reasons for doing so, as already noted.

Defining the Target. In the preceding example, the focus was on individual professionals. The reader may well have questioned how the professionals' clients stood to gain or lose by our decision. Are not recipients of professionals' services potential beneficiaries of continuing professional education, at least indirectly?

Such queries raise legitimate moral issues regarding the target of continuing professional education interventions. Chapter One differentiates between the individual, organization, and professional delivery system as potential targets for continuing professional education. From a sociological perspective, the revisionist viewpoints described by Cervero, Bussigel, and Hellyer in Chapter Two raise value-laden questions regarding the appropriate focus of continuing professional education intervention. Whether these perspectives are structural or sociological in orientation, they pose the fundamental moral dilemma of cui bono: To whose advantage should our efforts be directed?

The second situation presented in this chapter describes one such dilemma, a choice between professional development or client education needs. Given the setting, pure utilitarian reasoning would focus heavily on the comparative effectiveness of these methods in achieving the desired good of increased organizational effectiveness. Although such an approach could serve to promote the greatest good for the greatest number, it could still result in injustices in how this "sum" was distributed. The inequalities in service delivery described in this situation raise the issue of justice and, by implication, the issue of the "appropriate" target for intervention.

Applying formalist principles to this situation, the choice between professional development and client education represents a conflict between addressing the legitimate claims of the organizations' clients (the principle of justice) and pursing what the organization defines as in its best interests, namely the professional development of its staff (the principle of beneficence). As in the preceding case, resolution of the dilemma would be based on an established hierarchy of principles. A potentially confounding factor for the continuing professional education practitioner responsible for the decision would be his or her obligations and allegiance to the parties involved. Conflicting obligations and their potential as a source of value conflicts are addressed in a subsequent section.

Choice of Means. The choice of means used to implement an educational intervention lies at the heart of the teaching-learning process. Unfortunately and all too often, the ethical dilemmas inherent in teaching are obfuscated by simple dicta to ensure quality or perform one's role as professionally as possible (Scriven, 1982). This approach belies the fact that one's choice of or commitment to a particular teaching-learning method represents in part a moral conviction (Baumgarten, 1982).

Moral convictions regarding the choice of educational strategies evolve from the assumptions underlying the various goal orientations toward continuing professional education, as Chapter One shows. Analysis of these assumptions reveals a fundamental dichotomy in approach: The growth orientations tend to stress methods that encourage diverse forms of individual development, while the remedial and change orientations tend to emphasize means suited to the cultivation of objectivity and the acceptance of universal standards.

The inherent tension between these two general approaches is clearly evident in the third situation highlighted in this chapter. The educator is faced with the dilemma of choosing between a voluntary andragogical and a mandated behaviorally oriented approach to teaching. If clear scientific evidence supported one approach over the other, the choice would be more empirical than moral. However, because both approaches are value laden, the educator's choice must ultimately be based on moral reasoning.

As in the other examples, the pure utilitarian framework would weigh the projected value and disvalue resulting from selection of the available alternatives. As we have seen, the utilitarian calculus is confounded by our definition of intended beneficiaries, particularly when an organization or professional delivery system is the target of intervention. Nonetheless, pure utilitarian thinking is the most likely of all modes of ethical reasoning to support use of a questionable means to achieve a desired end, and in this particular situation it would probably justify the mandated intervention.

In contrast, the obligation-based approaches of formalism and rule utilitarianism would attempt to reconcile the conflict between the moral principles underlying each strategy. With the andragogical approach heavily founded on human freedom (Knowles, 1980) and the behavioral approach emphasizing compliant dependence, the choice of means must be based on resolution of the priority given to the principles of autonomy and beneficence.

Evaluating Consequences. Nowhere is the potential for conflict among values greater than in the process of evaluating the consequences of educational interventions. Perhaps more than their traditional academic counterparts, continuing professional education practitioners experience the tension inherent in assuming the various roles of evaluator, screener, certifier, and helper of their clientele. Moreover, on an administrative level, responsibilities for program evaluation raise a host of related ethical issues, as Chapter Five shows.

In regard to the obligations inherent in the evaluative role of continuing professional education practitioners, Davies (1981) identified three rights common to all learners: the right to privacy, the right to confidentiality, and the right to responsible assessment. These rights and the correlative obligations stem from both utilitarian and formalist conceptions of morality. From a rule utilitarian perspective, failure to uphold these precepts would compromise the trust implicit in our fiduciary relationships with learners and potentially make such interactions less effective or impossible. From a formalist perspective, these rights derive from and exemplify the principles of autonomy and justice; upholding them represents a prima facie duty.

The fourth situation presented in this chapter represents a classic dilemma of such rights in conflict. On the one hand, we are obligated to uphold the practitioner's right to privacy and confidentiality of evaluative information (the principles of autonomy and justice); on the other hand, we are held to ensure that the best interests of the public, such as preventing harm and promoting safety and welfare (the principle of beneficence), are realized. Compounding the dilemma is the legal precept regarding confidentiality; that is, the protective privilege ends where the public peril begins. Ultimately, the decision to maintain confidentiality or to release private records for public scrutiny depends on the agency's articulation of valued principles, its specification of intended beneficiaries, and the extent to which confidentiality of evaluative data is communicated to its clientele.

Issues related to program evaluation are broader in scope than client evaluation and beyond the focus of this chapter. Those who wish to pursue these issues can refer to Perloff and Perloff (1980) and Anderson and Ball (1978).

Organizational Sources of Value Conflicts. Confounding the sources of value conflicts arising by virtue of the role of continuing professional education as means of social intervention are its unique organizational characteristics. Foremost among the potential sources of value conflicts in continuing professional education are its common reliance on multiple linkages with external agencies and its business and marketing orientation. Both evolve from the marginal status that continuing professional education typically holds within the parent organization.

External Linkages. As Hohmann notes in Chapter Six, professional groups in general and continuing professional education providers in particular have become increasingly dependent on the financial and educational resources made available through collaborative linkage arrangements. Although there is nothing inherently unethical about such arrangements, multiple linkages can pose the problem of conflicting interests. A good example of the potential for such conflict is collaborative programming between a continuing professional education provider and a supporting industrial or commercial sponsor. Although industrial representatives may assert that their immediate motives are to assist in providing quality programming and that bottom-line benefits derive only secondarily from the goodwill established among members of the professional community, programming can be exploited for promotional purposes. Cognizant of this potential in continuing medical education, the Alliance for Continuing Medical Education Council (1983) adopted guidelines to ensure the integrity of joint programming efforts.

Stern (1982) has raised similar questions regarding the often tenuous balance struck between academic standards and the role of continuing professional education in academia. Stern's fundamental thesis is that the characteristically external orientation of continuing professional education to its constituencies does not need to be a source of conflict with traditional academic values and that providers can walk in the marketplace and keep their academic virtue.

Business Orientation of Continuing Professional Education. Some of the most common and difficult to refute claims regarding unethical practices in continuing professional education are related to the marketing and business perspectives that characterize the operations of many providers. At the heart of this product orientation is the fact that most providers depend on program revenues for continued survival. Given the voluntary nature of most participation in continuing professional education and the increasing competition among providers for a share of the limited market (Stern, 1983), it is little wonder that anecdotes of questionable business practices abound.

Most of these anecdotes focus on the use of nonrational persuasion, downright untruthfulness in promotion and advertising, or conflicts between educational quality and the bottom line, where revenue competes with expenditures. Fortunately, business itself has exhibited a long tradition of ethical inquiry into its theories and practices. Sound guidance in addressing these issues is provided by Beauchamp and Bowie (1979), Donaldson and Werhane (1979), and Regan (1984). As applied to the practice of continuing professional education, such perspectives support the claim that good education and good business (*good* in the moral sense of rightness) are not incompatible.

Conclusion

In its most primitive state, morality represents a culturally defined set of externally imposed principles on which an individual is expected to act. Higher levels of morality require that individuals internalize a rationally derived system of ethical reasoning and use it to guide and regulate their behavior in consistent ways. On an individual level, the choice of which system of thought to adopt ultimately depends on one's underlying value premises. However, those who choose to engage in helping relationships are obliged to transcend this individual orientation and incorporate both the language and the substance of human rights and obligations into their systems of reasoning.

Like many of the groups that it serves, continuing professional education is an occupation that aspires to professional status. Long ago, Socrates demanded that professionals acknowledge the social context of their activities and that they recognize their obligations toward the segment of society that they profess to serve. As our analysis of ethical reasoning has made clear, only by identifying, justifying, and prioritizing basic principles of human values can the planner or provider of continuing professional education resolve the difficult questions of moral behavior in consistent ways. To the extent that clearly articulated principles guide our choices and actions, all involved will be well served.

References

Alliance for Continuing Medical Education. *The Relationship Between Commercial Companies and CME Courses Presented by Medical Schools.* Rye, N.Y.: Alliance for Continuing Medical Education, 1983.

Anderson, S. B., and Ball, S. *The Profession and Practice of Program Evaluation.* San Francisco: Jossey-Bass, 1978.

Baumgarten, E. "Ethics in the Academic Profession: A Socratic View." *Journal of Higher Education,* 1982, *53,* 282–295.

Beauchamp, J. L., and Bowie, N. E. (Eds.). *Ethical Theory and Business.* Englewood Cliffs, N. J.: Prentice-Hall, 1979.

Callahan, D. "Should There Be an Academic Code of Ethics?" *Journal of Higher Education,* 1982, *53,* 335–344.

Chambers, C. M. "Foundations of Ethical Responsibility of Higher Education Administration." In R. H. Stein and M. C. Baca (Eds.), *Professional Ethics in University Administration.* New Directions for Higher Education, no. 33. San Francisco: Jossey-Bass, 1981.

Davies, I. K. *Instructional Technique.* New York: McGraw-Hill, 1981.

Dill, D. D. "The Structure of the Academic Profession: Toward a Definition of Ethical Issues." *Journal of Higher Education,* 1982, *53,* 255–267.

Donaldson, T., and Werhane, P. H. (Eds.). *Ethical Issues in Business.* Englewood Cliffs, N.J.: Prentice-Hall, 1979.

Frankena, W. K. *Ethics.* (2nd ed.) Englewood Cliffs, N.J.: Prentice-Hall, 1973.

Kelman, H. C., and Warwick, D. P. "The Ethics of Social Intervention: Goals, Means, and Consequences." In G. Bermant, H. C. Kelman, and D. P. Warwick (Eds.), *The Ethics of Social Intervention.* Washington, D.C.: Hemisphere, 1978.

Knowles, M. S. *The Modern Practice of Adult Education: From Andragogy to Pedagogy.* (2nd ed.) New York: Association Press, 1980.

Mason, R. C. "Managerial Role and Style." In P. D. Langerman and D. H. Smith (Eds.), *Managing Adult and Continuing Education Programs and Staff.* Washington, D.C.: National Association for Public Continuing and Adult Education, 1979.

Perloff, R., and Perloff, E. (Eds.). *Values, Ethics, and Standards in Evaluation.* New Directions for Program Evaluation, no. 7. San Francisco: Jossey-Bass, 1980.

Regan, T. (Ed.). *Just Business: New Introductory Essays in Business Ethics.* New York: Random House, 1984.

Ross, W. D. *The Right and the Good.* Oxford, England: Clarendon Press, 1930.

Scriven, M. "Professional Ethics." *Journal of Higher Education,* 1982, *53,* 307–317.

Singarella, T. A., and Sork, T. J. "Questions of Values and Conduct: Ethical Issues for Adult Education." *Adult Education Quarterly,* 1983, *33,* 244–251.

Stern, M. R. "Can You Walk in the Marketplace and Keep Your Academic Virtue?" *Mobius,* 1982, *2* (4), 54–65.

Stern, M. R. (Ed.). *Power and Conflict in Continuing Professional Education.* Belmont, Calif.: Wadsworth, 1983.

A health professional by background, Craig L. Scanlan has assisted numerous educational institutions, health care agencies, professional societies, and lay organizations in planning, implementing, and evaluating continuing education programs for their clientele.

Who are we? What do we do? Why do we do it? These
key questions must be addressed if continuing educators
are to confront the issues in meaningful ways.

Persistent Problems and Promising Prospects in Continuing Professional Education

William S. Griffith

The focus of this sourcebook has been limited to issues raised by the practice of individuals who use traditional programmatic delivery methods to
provide continuing professional education. The intent is to be complementary to and minimally duplicative of the existing literature on continuing professional education. Stern (1983) and Houle (1980) broaden the
perspective presented here. Stern's focus on organizational providers
addresses key questions regarding the responsibility for developing and
organizing continuing professional education. Houle's emphasis on the
characteristics of professionalization and its relationship to various modes
of learning treats formal continuing professional education as one of the
many factors that contribute to individual and collective professional development. Given the complexity of the issues and their interrelationships,
such resources as these provide a necessary accompaniment to the major
questions posed in this volume.

In addressing what they believe to be among the most salient issues
confronting continuing professional education, the contributors have raised

R. M. Cervero, C. L. Scanlan (Eds.). *Problems and Prospects in Continuing Professional Education.* New Directions
for Continuing Education, no. 27. San Francisco: Jossey-Bass, September 1985.

several key questions. Four of the questions that are most important and useful in analyzing the current problems and future prospects of continuing professional education are these: First, who are the continuing professional educators? Second, whose learning are they planning, guiding, and evaluating? Third, how is this learning to be accomplished? Fourth, on what content should this learning focus? Implicit in each of these questions is the question of why; that is, what purpose is continuing professional education intended to serve? Taken together, these questions provide the necessary framework for analyzing and addressing the major issues characterizing the field.

Who Are the Continuing Professional Educators?

In examining the current status of continuing professional education, a clear understanding of the populations being considered seems imperative. Several chapters in this sourcebook implicitly assume that all continuing professional educators have had academic preparation in the field of continuing education itself.

Continuing education may be thought of as a generic field of practice and research. Continuing professional education is a subspecialty of continuing education that focuses on programming for persons who have earned their professional qualifications in some field and who have subsequently sought additional educational experiences to remind them of what they once knew and have forgotten, to acquaint them with knowledge that has developed since they earned their qualification, and to help them solve personal and professional problems of various kinds.

Although data that could establish the extent to which continuing educators in the professions have actually pursued academic training in continuing education are not available, conversations with individuals employed as managers of continuing education in several professions leads me to conclude that the proportion of continuing professional educators who have had such training does not exceed approximately 5 percent. Accordingly, if one is thinking and writing about continuing professional educators, one is in fact thinking and writing about individuals who have not been academically prepared to assume their roles; that is, they have not been academically prepared to conceptualize, plan, conduct, and evaluate programs of continuing professional education.

Cervero, Bussigel, and Hellyer note in their examination of the relationship between continuing educators and the professions that an increasing but unspecified number of continuing educators are employed in positions that have heretofore been closed to them; these educators are acting as directors of continuing education in professional associations where only people trained in the profession itself used to serve.

Nonetheless, Kenny observes in Chapter Four that one reason why quality standards have emerged is that the individuals who have been placed in positions of educational responsibility within organizations involved in providing continuing professional education are often limited in their educational background and expertise. If Kenny is correct, then the increasing popularity of accreditation ought to be accompanied by an increasing awareness of the value of employing adequately prepared continuing education specialists as continuing educators in the professions.

Knox spells out a logical approach to evaluation in Chapter Five that may seem easy for an amateur educator to implement just because it is explained so clearly. Nevertheless, he reminds the reader that even the most proficient evaluators have difficulty documenting improvements in performance (and related benefits to others) that can be traced to participation in educative activity. Accordingly, conducting a sophisticated evaluation of continuing professional education appears to require a fair level of educational expertise.

At least three sorts of persons are involved in the planning, conduct, and evaluation of continuing professional education. The largest group, perhaps 95 percent of the total, is made up of individuals who have had their academic preparation in one of the specialty areas within the profession for which they are now planning, conducting, and evaluating continuing professional education. The second group, probably about 4.5 percent of the total, is made up of individuals who have not pursued academic preparation in any of the specialty areas within the profession that they are now serving; instead, they acquired their specialized knowledge entirely in the field of continuing education itself, and they have chosen to apply their skills and insights for the members of a particular profession. The third and smallest group is composed of persons who first acquired their qualifications in a given profession and subsequently invested the time required to acquire competence in the field of continuing education.

Individuals who have had their training entirely within a specific profession, such as veterinary science or orthopedic surgery, and who subsequently have been designated by an employer to plan, manage, and evaluate education are likely to regard their previous professional preparation as the basis for their distinction and to look for ways in which they can use their established professional expertise (of a noneducational nature) in the practice of their new responsibilities as an educator. To the extent that continuing professional educators focus their attention on developments in the field of continuing education, their knowledge of their former specialization is likely to become obsolete. It seems improbable that any but a few highly gifted individuals would be able to develop and maintain their competence in two professions simultaneously.

The fundamental question that the established professions must face is this: Can an individual who has been prepared academically as a continuing educator practice with equal facility in any professional setting? In a sense, what this question is asking is whether there is actually a profession of continuing education. To date, research has not compared the performance of continuing professional educators who were academically prepared in a profession before being assigned to their responsibilities as continuing educators with the performance of continuing professional educators whose academic training and experience were exclusively in the field of continuing education.

If we assume that approximately 95 percent of the persons working directly in the field of continuing professional education have not been prepared academically to perform their educational role, then we might well expect that they will have philosophical disagreements with the core of professionally prepared continuing educators who are writing and speaking about the purposes of continuing professional education. Accordingly, as Cervero, Bussigel, and Hellyer point out, there could well be continuing educators outside of continuing professional education who hold to social structural revisionist theories and who thus are at odds with continuing educators who believe that the professions are in fact intended to advance the welfare of clients, not to protect the vested occupational interests of the members of the profession. George Bernard Shaw observed that all professions are a conspiracy against the laity, a viewpoint that would not be acceptable to most continuing professional educators. It is difficult to imagine how a continuing educator who was convinced that professionalism is a means of protecting an occupation could work effectively within any of the settings in which continuing professional educators serve. Social structural revisionists could scarcely be expected to compromise their principles enough to plan, conduct, and evaluate programs that conflicted with their philosophical perspective. So, if there is a conflict between some continuing educators who are not working with professional groups and some who are, it might be traced to a deep-seated distrust of the professions among the former and to a basic feeling of trust in the professions among the latter.

Who Are the Intended Learners?

Disagreement about who the clients of continuing professional education are might seem impossible, but Cervero, Bussigel, and Hellyer have shown in Chapter Two that conceptually there can be marked differences of opinion. While the dominant and traditional viewpoint is that the individual professional is the target of continuing professional education programs, the view is now emerging that groups, rather than individuals, must be regarded as the learners if major changes are to be facilitated within the professions.

From a second perspective, Cervero, Bussigel, and Hellyer note that continuing educators who subscribe to a revisionist philosophy want to persuade both the professionals and their clients that their power should be equal. Because the revisionists see the ideology of professionalism as a means of occupational control, the educational programs that they plan should tend to focus on empowering the clients, not on improving the professionals' performance directly.

Scanlan noted in Chapter One that, although most continuing professional education has an individual orientation, it is coming to accept and to serve the needs of organizations and of society. The beneficiaries of educational programs now include the organization and the delivery system as well as the individual.

Hohmann expresses an interest in boundary spanners, individuals who serve as links between organizations. Because of her interest in inter-institutional collaboration, she argues that joint educational ventures involving two or more autonomous professional groups are likely to benefit all parties involved.

In his examination of the relationship between program planning and accreditation, Kenny points out that, although self-directed learners are not involved in institutionally sponsored programs, those who are concerned about accreditation have a responsibility to develop an acceptable system for the documentation of self-directed learning. This view enlarges the responsibility of the continuing education specialist to include not only those who enroll in formal educational programs but also those who engage in self-directed learning activities.

In his discussion of evaluation in Chapter Five, Knox acknowledged the difficulty of assessing the indirect benefits of participation by professionals for their clients. It might reasonably be argued that, even though the individual professional is usually the learner in continuing education programs, the most persuasive ground for providing educational opportunities to professionals is not the benefit accruing to them but rather the improved professional service that their clients are assumed to receive.

How Is the Education to Be Accomplished?

Since most practitioners of continuing professional education have prepared in fields other than continuing education, it is not surprising that the approaches they use to conduct and evaluate programs are more likely to reflect their particular predispositions than a considered examination of the range of possible methods that continuing educators could use. So, a consideration of methods, techniques, and devices led by a continuing education specialist could very well be of interest and utility to those who have been designated practitioners of continuing professional education by their employers.

In his examination of practice in continuing professional education,

Scanlan noted what he regards as an overemphasis on skills, means, and details to the detriment of principles, ends, and the big picture. He attributes the situation to confusion about goals and purposes and believes that the situation is unlikely to improve until some agreement is reached on a working philosophy for continuing professional education. The diversity of purposes results in a diversity of methods that reflects ambiguity and confusion rather than informed choices among carefully considered alternatives.

Although Kenny does not address questions of how decisions should be made about methods and techniques, he is quite clear in calling for continuing professional education across professions. In his view, an expert on continuing professional education is one who works on common concerns across professions and who has skills not only as an educator of adults but also as a manager of the information required to meet the standards of accreditation.

Like Kenny, Hohmann argues that the professions need to broaden their perspectives and address common issues and concerns. The method she identifies as useful in this regard, the Practice Audit Model, requires collaborative discussion and problem solving among diverse groups and organizations. Although the Practice Audit Model is more a planning tool than an instructional technique, it exemplifies what Houle (1980) has called the inquiry mode of learning.

In Chapter Five, Knox does not advise readers on the selection of methods and techniques. Instead, he emphasizes the importance of the use of sound evaluation processes in efforts to facilitate decision making.

None of the authors has chosen to discuss the importance of distinguishing between cognitive objectives and objectives that deal with attitude change. If a change is sought not just in the level of knowledge that professionals can demonstrate but in their behavior as well, then it seems reasonable to advocate that program designs, such as residential education, which have been reported to be effective in changing attitudes should be employed in preference to methods that are best suited to information transfer.

If the practitioners of continuing professional education are to move toward a more professional level of practice, an educational program must be mounted that is exclusively for them. None of the authors has addressed the value of such a program, and none has suggested that an in-service or short-term training program for these individuals should be a high-priority activity for the Commission of Professors of Adult Education, the American Association for Adult and Continuing Education, or any other association whose stated purpose is the improvement of continuing education practice. Since the area of specialization is continuing education, it seems reasonable to expect that those who have had the benefit of academic training and are convinced of its value should address the training or continuing education of continuing professional education practitioners.

What Is the Subject Matter to Be Taught?

Not all professions came to accept a need for continuing professional education at the same time. Because they have entered the field over a number of years, their experience in mounting continuing professional education programs varies. Further, even if most practitioners of continuing professional education have no training in the field, they are probably thoughtful people who have learned a great deal as a result of their experience in planning, conducting, and evaluating continuing education. Accordingly, the focus of their efforts might reasonably be expected to evolve over their years of practice. The variation in years of practice might explain some of the differences in the continuing education programs that the various professions offer. While some professions have accepted a degree of responsibility for personal development among their members, others have limited their educational ventures to remedial and updating kinds of programs.

All the contributors to this volume offer observations on the goals and choice of subject matter to be taught in continuing professional education programs. They note the evolution of purpose in continuing professional education and the implications of that evolution for the selection of appropriate content. Overall, it can be said that the authors see a need for programs that serve each of the evolving purposes.

Unique Aspects of Continuing Professional Education

Although continuing professional education has many characteristics in common with other forms of continuing education, it has some unique characteristics of its own. Continuing educators must have knowledge of these special aspects if they hope to work cooperatively with practitioners in continuing professional education. Grotelueschen points out that the tendency to generalize directly from research findings on continuing education in general to continuing professional education is likely to produce misleading results. He argues that the literature on participation in continuing education is not particularly helpful in assisting the practitioners of continuing professional education to understand and modify the behavior of those who are engaged in continuing professional education. Because continuing educators have typically noted that educational level, income, and occupation are the best predictors of the level of educational participation and because these are constants, rather than variables, within professions, the knowledge of who is participating in general con-

108

tinuing education programs and of why they are participating is of no use
to practitioners of continuing professional education. If research on participation in continuing education is to be of value to practitioners of
continuing professional education, Grotelueschen observes, then it must
concentrate not on the intended audience, most of whose members will not
appear for the programs planned with them in mind, but on improving
service to those who participate.

Conclusion

Compared with other sectors of the educational community, continuing professional education is still in an adolescent stage of development.
Clearly, both the rapid growth and the uncertainties characterizing that
period of maturation are evident throughout the field. As in human development, the natural tendency during this difficult stage is to question
one's purpose, to seek out new directions, and to refine one's conception
of self. Clearly, the contributors to this sourcebook are sensitive to these
evolving concerns, and they have provided ways that allow those involved
to begin addressing the orderly development and maturation of continuing
professional education. In such a context, it is wholly appropriate for this
concluding chapter to focus on guiding questions rather than on concrete
answers. Formulating answers to these questions will provide the sense of
purpose that continuing professional education needs in order to mature
and assume its rightful place as a full partner in the educational development of professionals. As this sourcebook illustrates, there are reasons to
be optimistic about the future of this exciting sector of continuing
education.

References

Houle, C. O. *Continuing Learning in the Professions.* San Francisco: Jossey-Bass,
1980.
Stern, M. R. (Ed.). *Power and Conflict in Continuing Professional Education.*
Belmont, Calif.: Wadsworth, 1983.

*William S. Griffith is professor of adult education at the
University of British Columbia. He has served two terms as
chairman of the Commission of the Professors of Adult
Education and been elected twice to the steering committee of
the Adult Education Research Conference.*

Index

A

Accounting: and collaboration, 78; goals of continuing education in, 11. *See also* Certified public accountancy
Accreditation: analysis of program planning for, 47–59; approaches to, 53; conclusion on, 58; and content relevance, 56–57; and education industry, 47–50; and learning assessment, 57–58; and learning objectives, 55–56; management of education for, 52; management of information for, 51–53; and program evaluation, 57; and promotional materials, 54–55; responsibilities for, 51–58; and standards of practice, 50–51, 54–58
Accreditation Council for Continuing Medical Education, 50, 58
Adult Education Association of the U.S.A. Task Force on Voluntary Learning, 22, 30
Alliance for Continuing Medical Education, 97, 98
Allied health services: goals of continuing education in, 11; and participation, 35
American Association for Adult and Continuing Education, 106
American Association for Respiratory Therapy, 53
American Association of University Professors, 88
American Council on Pharmaceutical Education, 53, 56–57, 59
American Dental Association, 14, 17, 53
American Institute of Real Estate Appraisers, 53
American Medical Association, 53; Physician's Recognition Award of, 49
American Nurses' Association, 53
American Psychological Association, 53
American Public Health Association, 53
American Society of Association Executives, 76

Anderson, R. E., 35, 44
Anderson, S. B., 63, 71, 96, 98
Anderson, W. A., 37, 44
Apps, J. W., 6, 7, 8, 17
Aquinas, T., 90
Architecture: and collaboration, 78; and mandation, 49
Aristotle, 90
Arons, A., 12, 17–18
Association of Continuing Legal Education, 53

B

Ball, S., 63, 72, 96, 98
Banking, goals of continuing education in, 12
Barrows, H. S., 67, 71
Baumgarten, E., 95, 98
Beauchamp, T. L., 97, 98
Becker, H. S., 66, 72
Beder, H. W., 76, 84
Belasco, J. A., 63, 69, 72
Beneficiaries: of continuing professional education, 13–14, 23–24, 36; defining, 94–95, 104–105; of standards, 50–51
Bergevin, P., 7, 18
Bloom, B. S., 57, 59
Boshier, R., 34, 44
Boundary spanners, in collaboration, 79–80
Bowie, N. E., 97, 98
Brown, C. R., Jr., 67, 72
Burgess, P., 34, 44
Burnford, F., 77–78, 84
Bushman, W. M., 10, 18
Business professionals, and participation, 35, 38, 41, 42
Bussigel, D., 1, 21–31, 75, 94, 102, 104, 105

C

Callahan, D., 88, 98
Catlin, D. W., 37, 38, 44
Certified public accountancy: and accreditation, 50; and continuing